BATTLES & BIVOUACS

BATTLES & BIVOUACS

JACQUES ROUJON,
FRED ROTHWELL

ISBN: 978-93-90294-69-5

Published: -

LECTOR HOUSE LLP
E-MAIL: lectorpublishing@gmail.com

BATTLES & BIVOUACS
A FRENCH SOLDIER'S NOTE-BOOK

BY

JACQUES ROUJON

TRANSLATED BY
FRED ROTHWELL

I' leur semble qu'i'faut parler de la Ramée, grenadier de Champagne, comme d'un prince dont auquel on ne risque rien de vanter toujours. I' vous lui mettent l'épée à la main qu'ça doit lui fatiguer le poignet furieusement et qu'on dirait qu'la Ramée n'a jamais fait autre chose d'aussi meilleur ... I'n'faut pas se battre tous les jours: i' n'y aurait plus de plaisir.

(LE CONTE DE LA RAMÉE.)

CONTENTS

BATTLES AND BIVOUACS

CHAPTER I

HUMES

Tuesday, 11th August, 1914.

Five o'clock in the morning. *En route* for the Gare de l'Est. All the same, as I turn the corner of the street in which I live, I experience a feeling of heartrending distress. I stop and glance back. Then I wave my hand to the window. Bah! I shall come back.

It is a fine, sunny day. There are crowds of people in front of the station — men of every description, most of them wearing caps, but no shirt-collar, some with *musettes*[1] slung over the shoulder, others carrying a valise. A few belonging to the ranks are wearing uniforms quite out of date. Any amount of bustle and noise but no shrieks. Those who stay behind remain with cheeks glued to the iron railings, their eyes fixed on some particular individual until he is out of sight.

On the platform I come across Verrier, a friend I have known all my life: at school, in the Latin Quarter, and during my military service. He is a tall, light-complexioned fellow, thin and pallid, very cool and self-possessed.

We find that we are both to be sent to the same depot.

As there are some seats unoccupied in a second-class carriage, we quickly take possession of them, delighted at the prospect of travelling elsewhere than on the floor.

The train begins to move. We look at each other.

"This time things are serious," remarks Verrier.

Indeed, we have something more to think of than passing exams, at school or college, or being reviewed by the colonel.

We spring to the window like the rest and shout out, "Vive la France!"

Henceforward all our thoughts must be directed towards peace — peace along the path of victory.

Our compartment is stiflingly hot. There are eight of us, belonging to every

---

[1] A *musette* is a kind of brown cloth satchel worn by a French soldier over the right shoulder and containing his rations, etc. — *Translator's Note.*

division of the service: artillery, cavalry, and infantry. Plunged suddenly into military life, we revive old memories and listen to interminable stories of stern adjutants and good-natured captains. A spirit of cordiality is immediately set up and at the same time a special brand of courtesy, for you have no idea to whom you may be talking; it is quite likely that the man in front of you will to-morrow be your corporal or your sergeant.

Every one of us is determined to do his duty; this is so manifestly taken for granted that no one mentions the matter. William II comes in for severe criticism.

"The whole thing's impossible. The Germans themselves will rise in revolt."

"They will do nothing of the kind," interrupts one who has lived in Germany. "They will do their best to kill us all."

"Whether they rise in revolt or not, they have Russia and England to deal with, and we also intend to do our share."

General approval. No one doubts but that the victory will be speedy—within three months, or before Christmas at the latest.

Provisions are distributed; we eat and drink. Toasts are passed. The train rumbles gently along; by noon we have only reached Villiers-sur-Marne. Along the whole length of the line stand people waving their handkerchiefs and wishing us good luck.

Our stops are frequent and prolonged. From time to time we jump down to stretch our legs a little. A red disc bars the way. Behind our train waits another, which sets up a loud strident whistle. The engine starts afresh. A few kilometres farther along, another stop. At the stations they offer us fresh, clear water in pails; they even offer us wine. Everything is very welcome.

It is sultry. Conversation begins to languish. Those who have a photograph of their children pass it round. We look at these portraits with the utmost sympathy and return them to the father, who apologizes for the fact that his eyes are brimming with tears.

Night descends. The men, half asleep, drowsily nod their heads or drop them gently on to their neighbours' shoulders.

Wednesday, 12th August.

About three in the morning we reach Langres. In the dimly lit station a thousand men are moving to and fro, asking questions. At the exit stand sub-officers, holding above their heads, at the end of a pole, large boards stating the numbers of the regiments. They collect their reservists and carry them off.

Is there no placard containing our number? What are we to do? I show my paper to an adjutant.

"The 352nd, 27th company? You must go to Humes."

"Humes! Where is that?"

"Have you come here for me to give you a lesson in geography? Find your way there as best you can."

A few paces away a detachment is forming: it is that of the 352nd. There are a hundred of us, and we are started along the road. Dawn appears. An hour and a half's march in silence. The men stagger along drowsily.

We reach Humes, a village five or six kilometres distant from Langres, situated in the valley of the Marne. The houses are low, with thatched roofs. The sergeant calls a halt in one of the streets.

Shortly we hear a commanding voice say—

"Second section, muster!"

Men issue from a shed near by, elbowing one another, some with and others without arms: this is the second section. They fall into line, form fours, and march off to drill, to the repeated call of one, two, one, two!

"Suppose we try to find the post-office?" says Verrier.

On reaching it, we each scribble a postcard and return to the street, wondering what to do next.

Before the sputtering tap of a street fountain stands a soldier at his ablutions, with bare breast, his red-trousered legs far apart. Of a sudden he gives a snort. I notice his closely cropped hair and his unshaven chin.

"Reymond!"

Reymond is a bosom friend of Janson's.

"I believe you're right," drawled Verrier. "We have not met for about a dozen years, so I don't suppose he'll recognize us."

Meanwhile, I call out—

"Hello, Reymond!"

The soldier stares at us from head to foot hesitatingly. We look like a pair of tramps, dirty and dishevelled, capless and collarless. Verrier affects a smoked eye-glass. Nevertheless, Reymond recognizes us.

"Ah! It's you, is it? *Chouette!*"

He has been here five days. Having been called up by mistake on the second day of mobilization, he was sent from Bernay to Langres, and then on to Humes.

"Come along, let's have a talk over a bottle," he says.

"What! Is there drink to be had at Humes?"

"Rather! The beer they drink in these parts will take a lot of beating."

Ten minutes afterwards one would think we had been the closest friends all our life. How fortunate to have come across Reymond! He is a painter, quite a gay companion, and possessed of that kind of assurance and self-confidence peculiar to certain bashful individuals. He is quite at home in the village, and carries us off to the office of our company. There he introduces us to the corporal, has our names enrolled in his squad, and supplies us with *gamelles*.

"I suppose you have had nothing to eat?" he asks.

"No."

"Come along with me."

He takes us to the cook.

"Here are a couple of men who feel peckish."

Our *gamelles* are filled and we sit down on the ground. We mess together and eat our share of the grub.

We are to receive our uniform to-morrow at the latest. Meanwhile, there is nothing left to do but wander about Humes. The Mouche is a pretty stream entering the Marne just on the outskirts of the village. There is a pool, a windmill, giant trees, and dung all over the place; cows and geese, poultry of every description, but few inhabitants. Soldiers abound.

At nine o'clock, Verrier, Reymond and myself make our bed in the hay. All around may be heard the usual jokes and pleasantries of the mess, just as in times of peace. One may distinguish the thick, rolling voices of those from Burgundy and the Franche-Comté, the accent of the Lyons silk-weavers, and the peculiar intonations of men from the various provinces. Bursts of laughter, then snoring followed by silence. Down below, in a stable, the plaintive lowing of a calf.

Thursday, 13th August.

Four in the morning.

"Time to get up!"

We shake and stretch ourselves. It is rather chilly.

The men come down from the loft on a tottering ladder which has one out of every two rungs missing.

In the street, the army cook, who has long been up and about, ladles coffee from a huge pot and fills the tins held out. In the tumult each man retires into a corner to avoid spilling the precious liquid.

Six o'clock. We are marched out of the village in columns of fours. The country is charming; the meadows through which flows the Marne are lined with poplars.

We return to quarters at ten o'clock. The sun's rays are beating down upon us. We baptize our street Dung Avenue.

Fortunately for us, the impossibility of isolating ourselves prevents us from thinking of what we have left behind. Here solitude and silence are unknown.

Friday, 14th August.

This morning we march twenty kilometres. The company collects in a meadow which a bend of the Marne has converted into a peninsula. During the tropical hours about noontime we indulge in a siesta beneath the faint shade of the poplars.

This life is an extremely healthy one; it constitutes a regular camping-out cure.

We now take our meals at the Hôtel du Commerce, kept by M. Girardot, nicknamed *Père Achille*. It is a large building on the main road between Paris and Belfort. Out in the yard and in both dining-rooms every table is engaged. Just as in the canteen, there is shouting and smoking, whilst the men call for drinks by hammering vigorously with their fists on the table.

Every evening amateur singers give us proof of their talent. The song relating the story of Suzette is a very popular one. No sooner is the last verse ended than *"Bis! bis!"* is roared out, and a willing encore is forthcoming. The artist raises his hand to his mouth and coughs, before recommencing, and every one joins in the chorus. The smoke rising from the pipes casts a dim mist over the lamps which hang from the ceiling.

Saturday, 15th August.

Père Achille places his loft at our disposal, at the farther end of the yard, above the stable. Climbing a ladder, you find bundles of hay to right and left. In the centre is a large open space containing a folding-bed occupied by Vitrier, of the 28th company, a neighbour and friend of the proprietor.

Here we shall get along quite comfortably, all the more so as we have also the run of a garden. There is an apple-tree, beneath whose shade we spend our leisure hours. Four stone steps enable us to go down to the river to wash our clothes or our persons. After all, cleanliness is a very simple matter, so far as we are concerned.

I have just seen the lieutenant in command of our company, and have given him my name. I am to leave with the next detachment which joins up, either with the regiment in reserve or with that in the field, according as the one or the other is the first to need reinforcements. This war will certainly not last long; we must hasten to reach the firing line if we could see anything of it.

What can be the matter? Letters take five or six days to arrive from Paris. The only journals we see are those of Langres: the *Petit Haut-Marnais* and the *Spectateur*, nicknamed at Humes *Le Secateur*. We crowd around the cyclists who bring them and clear off their supplies in a few moments.

The Paris journals have altogether stopped.

Sunday, 16th August.

The company musters at seven in the morning; the four sections, each in two rows, forming a square around the lieutenants and sub-officers.

The lieutenant in command is a kind-hearted man, on whom the gravity of the situation weighs heavily. This morning he declares curtly—

"The musters take far too long!"

Profound silence.

"Far too long. And I don't wish to speak of the matter again...."

Gabriel reads the daily orders: "Every morning, drill and marching. Tuesdays and Thursdays, rifle practice. Afternoons, lectures in quarters from one to three;

afterwards, Swedish gymnastics."

This existence in the depot, a blend between barrack-life and drill, will not be so very pleasant every day. May the powers that be send us speedily to battle!

This morning, at nine o'clock, military mass.

The church is situated on an eminence above Humes. Once the threshold is crossed, profound silence. Silence in broad daylight! Well, well! It rather puts one out!

There are flags around the walls. All the seats are occupied by soldiers and officers, *pêle-mêle*. A few peasant women are present, their sombre garments clashing with the blue and red uniforms.

It is a musical mass, and the music is worthy of a cathedral: all the instrumentalists and singers of the depot have had their services requisitioned. How striking the contrast between this grave ritual and ceremonial, the successive chants and breaks of silence, and the rough, stirring military life we have been spending for several days past, made up of shouts and hay, of cattle and dung.

A young priest has passed a surplice over his soldier's coat. His words are mild and kind, his sermon straight to the point, as he pleads the claims of family and country. The listeners weave their own dreams around his simple words as they fall upon the attentive and thoughtful assembly.

The end of the mass brings with it a change; these men, who have suddenly been unexpectedly moved in spite of themselves, make up for an hour's silence and immobility by shouting aloud and hustling one another.

Back at the hotel, with the aid of pipe and beer, they laud to the skies the priest's eloquence.

Big Albert, for whom it has been impossible to find a pair of pants large enough in the stores, wipes his mouth with the back of his hand after he has emptied his glass, and says—

"Believe me or not, as you please, but when that little priest spoke of our mothers and wives and children, well! I could no more keep back the tears than a woman!"

And there he stands, with legs outspread and hands in pockets, his vest unbuttoned over his protruding paunch. Evidently *he* is not subject to nervous attacks.

Reymond, Verrier and myself have obtained a pass for Langres. Lunch at the hotel; napkins and tablecloth. What luxury! The young lady who serves us is very polite. We enter various shops to purchase chocolate, wax candles, writing-paper, blacking, a lantern and some of Molière's plays to read aloud in the loft.

We return to Humes at six o'clock, shouting out songs at the top of our voice as the rain comes pouring down.

Monday, 17th August.

Five hundred men have been appointed to make up a detachment which is to hold itself in readiness to leave for the front at a minute's notice. My name is on the list, which includes men of the youngest classes and volunteers. It forms the contingent complement.

We are fitted out from head to foot. First, we receive a blue muff with which each man immediately covers his *képi*. This is the rallying sign. Out in the streets, comrades who see us wearing a blue *képi* say—

"Ah! So you are one of the complement?"

We answer, "Yes," in a tone of modest indifference ill concealed by a big dose of vanity.

A score of times every day we receive the order: "Those belonging to the contingent complement are wanted with everything they have at the office."

There we receive small packets of provisions, such as coffee, sugar, condensed soup; on another occasion, a *musette*; then again a can, leathern straps, cartridges; for each separate article of our equipment a special journey is necessary.

Such incidents as the following are quite common.

A man enters the office of the company, salutes, and says—

"Beg pardon, sergeant, but I have no sling for my rifle"; or, "I have no strap for my can"; or, "I have no suspension hooks."

The sergeant, busy writing, answers his interrupter—

"Will you go away! And quick, too!"

The man disappears, as the sergeant remarks to the company generally—

"Silly fellow, to come and ask me for straps whilst I am distributing *musettes!*"

You are asked for the number of your rifle, your full name and address. Then you go to the bureau for your identification disc, your first field-dressing, and lastly you are called upon to give the names and addresses of those to whom information must be sent in case of death. Ah! This is something we had never thought of.

Three legal functionaries and five sergeants, without counting the quartermaster, scribble away as fast as they can.

Again we are mustered, and the lieutenant sees us arrive one by one. With a despairing gesture, he asks—

"You call this a muster, do you?"

The contingent complement gathers round the door, waiting. At first whispering goes on, then voices are raised, there is jest and laughter. Suddenly a sub-officer leaves the sanctum.

"Stop this awful noise, will you! One can't hear oneself speak. Besides, what do you want here, lounging about the door? Off you go!"

We disappear, though not for long. Within a very few minutes an orderly is seen hurrying about and shouting—

"Quick! You are wanted at the office."

The sub-officer who has just dismissed us from the doorstep greets us with the words—

"Come, now, how is it that the men of the contingent complement are never to be found? Has some one to come and take you by the hand?"

Rain has been falling ever since the previous day. Humes is now a marsh; the river overflows its banks.

Tuesday, 18th August.

It is again fine. The contingent complement is back from march and drill, and I am resting on a form. All around is a regiment of hens and geese, geese with blue eyes just like those of a lady I once met and whom I suddenly call to mind.

The ducklings waddle along in twos, plunge their beaks and roll about in the liquid manure, and when they have become transformed into little balls of filth, they march away with the utmost gravity to gargle and clean themselves in the river. Farther away are cows, sheep, and dirty children. In front of me lie heaps of dung, two on my right and one on my left; it is quite unnecessary for me to turn round, for I am certain there is another behind me. The glorious sun, however, compensates for everything, and the scenery is very picturesque.

I spring to my feet as I hear the words: "The contingent complement is wanted at the office."

I cross the meadow, pass the river by the narrow drawbridge, and ascend the pebbly road leading to the shed euphemistically called "the office." A gift: ninety-six cartridges; a piece of news: the contingent complement is expected to leave for the front at any moment.

Both the gift and the piece of news are very welcome.

Then follow musters upon musters; reviews by corporal, sergeant, chief of section; review by the lieutenant in command of the company.

That evening, in the loft, Verrier and Reymond, who are to stay behind at Humes, minutely check the contents of my haversack and *musette*. They add a tin of preserves and complete my first field-dressing and sewing materials. Evidently they think that those in the fighting line run considerable risks. My own thoughts are all of home, after the war, of the peace and quiet of daily existence once this task is over.

Vitrier, the fortunate possessor of a folding-bed, returns at nine o'clock. The lucky fellow evades all the drills and marches, and spends his days at home in the neighbourhood. He is a charming person, whom we have affectionately nicknamed "the Spy," because he is to be met with only after twilight or before dawn. "The Spy" has brought young Raoul up to the loft; a gentle, light-complexioned, pallid-looking youth. He talks like a book and is full of such aphorisms as—

"For a man who, like me, is horrified at the very thought of death, a soldier's life is quite a mistake."

As he removes his foot-gear, Raoul tells us that he has been this afternoon watching the trains full of wounded pass by.

"My walk had a definite purpose, you see," he adds.

Down below, we hear the faint tinkling of a bell, suspended from the neck of an enormous dog, which we have nicknamed the *chien à sonnettes*.

In spite of his manifestly gentle disposition, this animal fills us with terror. He is always lying stretched at the foot of the ladder, and frequently in the dark we step on his head. To our amazement, he has bitten no one, so far.

Thursday, 20th August.

Is this the last réveillé in the loft? It has become a very comfortable spot. In the hay, where I lie wrapped up in a quilt, with a cotton nightcap coming over my ears, I would gladly sleep on into the middle of the morning. But it is five o'clock, and we must rise.

Drill and march. In the afternoon, siesta and conversation beneath the apple-tree. The weather is gloriously fine. We wash our socks in the Mouche.

Reymond has managed to secure an order; the lieutenant says to him—

"Since you are a painter, paint my name on my canteen."

He takes advantage of this diversion to avoid drill. He paints two white letters every day, and even then....

Friday, 21st August.

When is the contingent complement to leave? Armed for war, we have seen nothing but the office. It's not enough.

A change in our existence: the arrival of Lieutenant Roberty at Humes, and his appearance in our clan.

The other day, at muster, there was a rumour abroad that we were soon to have a new sub-lieutenant from Alsace. Here he is, in the centre of the square; of medium height, *papier mâché* appearance, very dark moustache, and the half-closed eyes of a myope. He wears red trousers and an extraordinary black coat, chimney-corner style, with a little gold lace at the sleeves. I look curiously at him, wondering where the deuce I can have seen that profile, so reminiscent of a tame jaguar.

A voice calls me; it is that of the new sub-lieutenant.

"Don't you recognize me?" ...

"No, *mon lieutenant*, and yet ... really, I cannot remember your name...."

"Roberty."

Raising my hands, I say—

"I beg your pardon, I have never seen you except in a dress suit."

And indeed, I remembered on the occasion of more than one general rehearsal the elegant appearance of my confrère. Comparing to-day's silhouette with that of former times, I simply remark—

"What a change! You look better in civilian clothes."

Instead of getting angry with me he merely laughs. A few comrades approach. As Roberty has just come from Alsace, he tells us of the first attack on Mulhouse, in which he took part.

"They say," remarks some one, "that the Germans scamper off as soon as they see the French?"

"That's what they say at the depot, is it? Well, since you are about to leave for the front, you will see for yourselves."

Roberty is bored to death at Humes, though he tolerates the Hôtel Girardot, with its garden and loft. He forgets his rank, and spends his leisure time with us. Discipline has already gained such a hold on us that at first we feel uneasy at such intimacy with a lieutenant. But really it is impossible to keep one's distance with Roberty. And now we have an additional comrade under the apple-tree or under the spiders' webs in the loft.

News at last. The French have had to fall back in Alsace. A big effort, however, is soon to be made in the north. The Russians have crossed the Prussian frontiers. In spite of slight impediments, things continue to go well.

Saturday, 22nd August.

By flattering the quartermaster I have had my haversack, which was slightly worn, exchanged for a new one. I put my things in it with the contented feeling of one who has managed to purchase a glass cupboard after years of economy.

How calm it is to-day! In the corner where I have taken refuge with my writing materials geese are gobbling up haricots under my very feet, as pleased as Punch at their daring.

The youths of Class 14 appear on the scene; they are mostly from the Vosges.

We tell them—

"Hullo, young ones! The war will be over before your training is finished."

They agree with the sentiment, though vexed to think it may be true. And they assure us they would do everything required of them, if called upon, just as well as the older men.

"All the same," we reply, "you can't expect us to want the war to continue merely to enable you to give an exhibition of your talents!"

CHAPTER II

IN LORRAINE

Sunday, 23rd August.

This morning we started in the direction of Belfort. About midnight the whole of Humes was peacefully sleeping when the bugler sounded a prolonged call, repeated all over the village. In a twinkling we join our squads. It appears that the regiment at the front urgently needs reinforcements of five hundred men.

The complement—no longer contingent—has mustered in the dark. After the roll-call we are summoned to the office for the last time. Distribution of rations and small loaves.

At six o'clock the five hundred are ready to start. Our chief is a lieutenant of the reserve—a schoolmaster in civil life. Each man has picked a few flowers on the roadside to fasten a bunch to his rifle. The whole depot is present. Verrier and Reymond give me a vigorous handshake. Really the whole scene moves me, though for nothing in the world would I have it appear so.

"Look out, there! Number! Form fours! Right wheel! Forward!"

The column begins to move, and we thunder forth the *Marseillaise* with the utmost enthusiasm. I turn round to wave a last farewell to my friends.

They return the gesture and shout, *"Au revoir!"*

At Langres station we enter the train, which rumbles off in an easterly direction. I again have the luck to find myself in a second-class carriage. The same atmosphere and gaiety as when we left Paris for the depot. Almost all my companions have gone before their turn. They are convinced they will come back and see the end of the business. And they wish to be in at the victory. The heat is terrible.

Perspiration trickles down faces already bronzed by a fortnight in the open air. There are ten in the compartment; all the same, at nightfall, we manage to drop off to sleep.

Monday, 24th August.

Daybreak. The road is blocked; we advance but slowly, stopping several times in the course of an hour. We almost run into a locomotive and three carriages that have been overturned, the result of a recent catastrophe.

During the night we have changed direction: instead of continuing towards the east, Gerardmer and the Schlucht, at Laveline we were shunted on to the line of Saint-Dié—Lunéville, across the Vosges. In the distance to the right we hear the roar of the cannon.

Raon-l'Etape. All change! It is noon. To the east of the station is a semi-circle of mountains. In the direction of the Donon the cannonade is incessant, though it no longer forms a dull rumble: each shot is distinct from the rest. Of their own accord the men load their rifles. We fall back upon Rambervillers.

It appears that things here are not progressing at all well. The 13th Corps, the van of which had reached Schirmeck, is now retreating before enormous forces. We see regiments file past: men and beasts look grimy and thin; there is a feverish look in their eyes, beneath the grey lids.

The artillery pass along so exhausted that they totter in their saddles; they have their ammunition-wagons behind them, but no guns.

Jokingly one of our men calls after them, not thinking what he is saying—

"Well, well! where are the cannon?"

Then they give us black looks and shrug their shoulders. Some one jerks his thumb over his shoulder in the direction of the enemy. We insist no further.

The men of the 13th Corps, who have been under fire for a fortnight without a break, see from our blue muffs, which still retain their colour, and from our comparative cleanliness, that we have just come on the scene. They call out to us—

"You new ones there have come at the right moment. You'll find plenty to do!"

An endless file of inhabitants fleeing before the invasion; they have heaped their goods and furniture on to great carts drawn by oxen, whilst they themselves follow behind, laden with baskets and bundles of all sorts.

For a few minutes a young woman walks along abreast of our section. She is carrying a little girl, whilst another hangs on to her dress. On a perambulator, which she pushes along, are piled up clothes and various odds and ends.

All these poor folk, seeing us proceeding in the direction of the west, know what it means: their homes abandoned, to be pillaged and burnt by the enemy.

Women cry out to us—

"This is the direction you should be taking, not that."

And they point eastwards. They even add—

"Are you running away?"

The road mounts and descends through woods of fir-trees. A lieutenant of dragoons is sleeping on the side of a copse, his arm linked in his horse's bridle. To the right is a dense mass of smoke, occasionally broken by red glares of light: Baccarat is in flames. A pitiless sun beats down on all this misery and sadness. The cannon roars incessantly. A sound as of thunder is heard, doubtless coming from the fort of Manonvillers. Night falls, and the sky is lit up with flashes of light. An aeroplane darts past, quite close to the ground. Without waiting for the word of command, the whole detachment fires at it.

Rambervillers is now in sight. We halt on the road. Prolonged discussion between the lieutenant and a staff officer.

The lieutenant comes up to us—

"We are on the wrong track; all the same we shall lay in a store of provisions and spend the night in the barracks of Rambervillers."

It is now quite dark. We wait in a barrack yard, until finally the lieutenant says that we may enter the buildings. Meat is passed round. I have not the heart to cook and eat a piece. Since the previous morning, twenty-four hours on the railway and thirty kilometres on foot, in the heat of the sun. However new and fresh we may be as troops, a little sleep is more than welcome.

Each man busies himself in finding quilt and straw mattress. The cannon are silent. For supper I dip some bread in my wine. It tastes good.

Tuesday, 25th August.

Three in the morning. Everybody is up and about. How I should have liked to sleep a few hours longer! In the yard, by candle-light, the lieutenant presides over a distribution of coffee, haricots and potatoes. Our *gamelles* must be taken down, filled and replaced on our haversacks.

What is the direction we are to take? The east, in all probability. We halt at dawn by the side of a wood and make some coffee. Fires are lit and the pots begin to boil. Some of us make an attempt to roast a piece of raw meat at the end of a stick, when the order comes to start off once more. We swallow the burning liquid. The lieutenant informs us that the detachment is to be linked on to the left of the 105th. The cannonade is intense. In a few moments we shall be within the line of fire. Everybody is in the best humour imaginable.

Now we are led along in a general movement, the purpose of which we naturally understand nothing; we have only to obey and keep our eyes open. Though full of spirit, we are quite bewildered and dumbfounded. In the first place, we expected to link up with our regiment; it appears that this regiment is fifty kilometres away. Then again, we are without officers: before leaving the depot, the detachment was divided into eight provisional sections of sixty men each. Several of these sections are commanded by a corporal, or even—a still more serious matter—by two corporals; it is so in our own case.

We traverse a hilltop and look down into a valley. The sections advance at intervals of thirty paces, in columns of fours. So far everything has been as regular as at an ordinary drill. The lieutenant sends an order that we are to halt and lie down. Good! It is fine, and the sun is beginning to make itself felt. Soon the entire section is lying stretched on the ground.

In front, a hill behind which the battle is being fought. The panting of the *mitrailleuses* may be clearly distinguished, by reason of its regularity, from the intermittent rending and tearing of musketry discharges. Suddenly a shell bursts, a distance of two hundred yards away. The cloud of black smoke rises and disperses almost immediately. Then come other shells at regular intervals. Are we the enemy's target? No. His object is to reach a village on our right and a wood of fir-trees on our left; the black clouds appear in turn over a house in the village, near the church steeple, over the wood. Suddenly, from the edge of the wood, four thunderous claps go off. Shouts of joy, as the section exclaims—

"Those are our 75's replying!"

They are speaking now in all directions. We are greatly excited, for every one is delighted at the spectacle of a real battle obtained so cheaply. No one is afraid. Not a single heroic word is uttered; merely rapid interjections.

"Ah! What a pity! There goes the steeple!"

And indeed, the steeple falls crashing to the ground as though it were no more substantial than a child's toy. It must surely have been made of cardboard to have crumpled up so quickly.

Still lying at full length on the grass, I pick a couple of flowers and place them in my pocket-book as a souvenir. Are we to spend the whole day basking in the sun?

The other sections rise and advance; we do the same. We make our way towards a wood over the hill opposite.

We skirmish along a road, beneath the firs. Near a tree, a dragoon, his breast bare and feet firmly planted on the ground, is having his back examined by a major; on his shoulder-blade is a large gash, from which the blood is dripping as from a tap. On the ground, by the wounded man's side—this is the first wounded soldier I have seen—lie his helmet and his arms, his coat and shirt.

The roar of battle increases; it is as though invisible hands were beating away with huge sticks on a number of carpets. We think we recognize the enemy's *mitrailleuses* by their *tacotacotac*, which continues for several seconds; whereas ours stop, begin again, stop once more, in less mechanical fashion.

The roar of our 75's may be distinguished amid the deafening crash; they go off in fours, with a sharp, clear crack.

The lieutenant arrives. We ask him—

"Where are the others?"

It is not his mission to tell us, but rather to send us over to a battery which is calling for infantry support.

The four cannon are close at hand, small, and with mouth pointing upwards. They have not been marked, fortunately for the gunners and for ourselves as well. The lieutenant is on the watch a few yards away, and we hear the words of command. The enemy is drawing nearer; a short time ago he was 2,400 yards away, then 2,000, and now he is within 1,800 yards.

Soon the captain of the battery gives the order—

"Bring up the limbers!"

The horses are a little to the rear, in a hollow of the meadow. The guns are now silent; they are fastened to the carriages. In a few minutes they have all left. It is ten o'clock. And what of ourselves?

An artilleryman passes along on horseback at a walking pace.

Some one asks—

"Why is the battery going away? Are we beaten?"

He flings at us the mild though superior look of a horseman for a foot-soldier.

"The Germans are firing at us from a distance of twelve kilometres with their 210's. It's right enough waging war, but not when the advantage is all on one side."

And off he goes. I look back and see him tossing his head.

A staff officer comes up at a gentle trot.

"What are you all doing here?" he asks.

"Artillery supports, *mon capitaine.*"

"Don't you see that your artillery is gone? You had better do the same. We are falling back."

From the crest the section descends into a smiling valley, through which winds a stream. A hostile aeroplane flies right above us; it drops a fuse in the form of a smoking serpent.

Ironical exclamations—

"What's that filth? Just look at it!"

Five minutes afterwards violent explosions are heard just overhead. The German artillery is peppering our retreat. Why is no one either killed or wounded? I cannot tell. A shell bursts right in the middle of a group of hussars, who disappear in the smoke. When it lifts, we see that both men and horses have been thrown to the ground, but they rise intact. Then every one within a radius of three hundred yards laughs.

We cross the river one by one on a plank. A couple of stretcher-bearers carry off a light-infantryman all covered with blood; his face is livid, beneath the dust and perspiration. His head shakes loosely about on the stretcher, and his eyes wear a dull, indifferent expression.

A few splinters fall harmlessly around. Assuredly the Germans are firing too high. I hear the remark—

"Their artillery is no good, and they aim no better than a peasant could do."

Noon. An implacable sun in a sky of crude blue. A glorious summer, really!

The 75's begin again. Their silence was somewhat disturbing.

We have been retiring for a couple of hours, and now we come to a halt. Why is this? If the Germans have beaten us, why do they not follow up their advantage? But then, in war a foot-soldier must resign himself to the fact that he may not know why he advances or withdraws. He sees only his immediate surroundings, nothing of any consequence.

The guns are silent. Not a shot is heard. The order is given to pile arms. We proceed to a neighbouring stream to quench our thirst and refresh ourselves by dashing a few quarts of water over our heads. No shade anywhere to be seen; we shall have to lie down in the full glare of the sun. Each couple shares a box of tinned meat, which is spread between pieces of bread. A refreshing drink is followed by a good smoke.

A hussar, galloping towards us, exclaims —

"Castelnau is here. We shall soon have them caught as in a vice!"

"Good!"

For some moments the lieutenant has been in conversation with a general. He now comes up and gives the order to pick up our arms. Our turn has come at last.

The general approaches.

"You are fresh troops," he says, "and I rely on you to do your best to capture the positions we lost this morning. Reinforcements are announced. What we have to do now is to gain time."

We ask for nothing more than to march forward. From time to time I catch the general's orders to the lieutenant: "Cross that village ... pass the bridge ... reach the heights ... make sure that the wood on the right is not occupied by the enemy ... do not lose contact with the main body...."

We advance in fours. Each section moves along in the same direction at intervals of a hundred yards. The lieutenant — the only officer for these five hundred men — marches at the head of my squadron.

On reaching the village mentioned, we find a peasant quietly leading three oxen to the watering-place. A little farther along two children, hand in hand, watch us file past. The houses are empty.

Once again the open country. Passing under an apple-tree, I pluck an apple and eat it to quench my thirst.

We cross a bridge. There are three roads before us. The lieutenant hesitates for a moment and then takes the middle one. No firing anywhere; perfect calm and silence.

On reaching an elevation, we are greeted with a storm of bullets.

I hear the orders to form a skirmish line, and to set our rifles at the 800 yards range.

Very soon we are being fired at from the front and from both sides. The lieutenant runs the entire length of the skirmish line. He brings the men forward in tens, according to regulations. I watch him and feel certain that he will be shot. No, he continues his course right in the thick of the bullets.

If only we could see the enemy! But he is safe in his trenches or hidden in the wood, and is able to fire at us as he pleases.

Lying flat on the grass, for the first time we hear the bullets whistle past. The enemy's fire, too well directed, sends the earth leaping into the air all around me. I imagine my head to be as large as a pumpkin. What a target! Whilst reloading, I notice an ant right in front of me, scaling some cartridge cases, and the thought comes to me—

"What an advantage to be quite small."

Hearing a cry, I turn my head and see a poor fellow with the blood streaming from his hand. The wounded man groans—

"*Aie! Aie!* Just what I expected!"

Then he stands upright. He feels that he has paid his debt and is now out of the game. It no longer interests him, so off he goes. He proceeds about a dozen yards towards the rear, and then, of course, falls dead to the ground, riddled with bullets.

The soldier on my right says—

"Now I'm hit!"

"Where?"

"A flesh wound in the arm. Nothing serious."

I am inquisitive enough to ask—

"Does it hurt?"

"I don't feel anything. For the moment there was a burning sensation. My arm is quite stiff."

It is the turn of his other neighbour to ask—

"Shall I dress it for you?"

"No, thanks. I had better get back to the rear."

"In that case, hand me your cartridges."

"Of course. I was forgetting."

The wounded man turns over on to his side, and with the bullets hailing down, quietly begins to empty his cases. His wound troubles him considerably, and he apologizes for his awkwardness.

"How numb my hand feels!"

Rules are rules, and regulations are regulations. Both soldiers have learnt, long ago in barracks, that sharpshooters advance in couples. They know that when one is wounded, the other must dress the wound, if possible, and in any case take the wounded man's cartridges. They think this is an opportunity to put into practice what they have learnt in theory. But what they do not know—and assuredly I am not going to undeceive them—is that the regulation they are following out was repealed over two years ago.

A comic interlude. A man, in a panic of fear, refuses to advance. A bugler, who has just been ordered to take command of the section, addresses him as follows—

"Forward! or you shall taste the butt-end of my rifle."

Groans and lamentations.

Then the bugler rises to his feet and says—

"Join your comrades ahead."

The other, utterly cowed, begins to crawl along the ground.

"No crawling! On your feet at once; I'll teach you to show the white feather!"

"You want me to be killed!"

"If you don't go at once, I'll kick you."

He gets up, whining and blubbering. The bugler accompanies him right to the line.

"Now lie down!"

The bugler, too, sinks to the ground. It is a miracle they were not both killed.

Meanwhile, the German artillery is beginning to find its mark. We pay heavily for every step forward; soon all advance is impossible. We are even compelled to retire when the *mitrailleuses* are directed upon us.

After our leaps forward we now have to leap backward. A few yards in a declivity afford us a moment's respite, the balls passing over our heads. Taking advantage of this, I open my *musette*, hoping to enjoy a drink, and find that a bullet has smashed the bottle to pieces. Now we have to climb some rising ground, the German bullets following us all the way.

The command is heard—

"Fix bayonets! the enemy is in the village. We are outflanked!"

Is this to be a hand-to-hand encounter? Nothing of the kind; the village is empty. The bayonets are sheathed.

Flinging our rifles over our shoulder, we turn away, firmly persuaded that, after traversing another hundred yards and finding ourselves once again in the open, we shall all be shot.

A wounded man, who has preceded us, calls to us as we pass. He is on his feet, though pale as death. His head is bandaged; there is a fixed glare in his eyes. The death sweat streams down his face, as he says hoarsely—

"You're not going to leave me here, are you? Take me away! I am wounded in three places."

"Come along, then; we'll carry you into this farm."

"No, no! They'll come and finish me. Please don't leave me behind."

One cannot tell the poor fellow that he will be dead before the Germans arrive. It is courting death for ourselves also, sure enough, but we take him tenderly by the arm and drag him away with us. Very speedily the end comes, and we leave him lifeless on the ground.

It is six o'clock. What remains of the section is crossing a field of oats. The bullets still follow us, also occasional bursts of artillery firing. We have to pass in and out of the projectiles like ants making their way between drops of water trickling from the rose of a watering-pot. The man by my side falls to the ground and lies there motionless.

Behind me I hear the snort of a shell.

"That one's for me!" I say to myself.

Instinctively I hitch up my haversack over my head. The shell explodes, and I am lifted into the air. Then I find myself flat on the ground. A stifling feeling comes over me; I tear off my cravat, coat and equipment, and I know no more.

It is night before I regain consciousness. Where am I? I stagger to my feet, but immediately sink to the ground like a drunken man. Rain is falling, thin but penetrating. The ground on which I lie stretched is a veritable quagmire. I perceive that my shirt and trousers form my only covering. My senses are quite confused; surely the whole thing is a horrible nightmare!

I am shivering all over, and my mouth is full of blood. What am I doing here all alone in the middle of the night, and half undressed? I feel myself all over; not a scratch. My watch and knife are in their place. After all, I am not dreaming. Then memory suddenly returns: the skirmish-line, the withdrawal under fire, the shell. I look around: everywhere on the horizon flames are to be seen. An occasional boom of cannon in the distance. I must have fallen between the lines.

Forward, straight in front of me, come what may. I cross a wood, and fall into a stream, where I remain for some time in an almost fainting condition.

The rumbling of carriage wheels makes me prick up my ears. I blindly feel my way in the direction indicated; I have lost my glasses. A short-sighted person without his glasses is in the mental condition of a drowning man. I am at the end of my tether. For three hours I have been crawling along; the rumblings draw near. Soon I hear the sound of voices; my heart stands still! What if the language is German! A good French oath reaches my ears. I run forward; the ground slips from beneath my feet, and I tumble headlong down a steep path into the midst of a convoy of stretcher-bearers.

They bundle me into a pair of blankets, as I am now quite helpless. I ask what time it is: three in the morning. I must have been unconscious from six o'clock till midnight.

Wednesday, 26th August.

At daybreak we reach Rambervillers. A major procures for me a *képi* and an odd coat, and sends me to the hospital.

My one object now is to find a pair of spectacles. The streets are almost deserted. A few groups here and there, in one of which I notice a man wearing an eyeglass. Going up to him, I speak of my difficulty. Sympathetic and understanding, he takes me to an optician. All the shops are closed: for one reason, because it is seven in the morning; for another, because, as I am informed, yesterday's battle did not turn well for us—I suspected this from what happened to myself—and the Germans might enter Rambervillers to-day. Here is the optician's place; he has left the town, and his wife is on the point of abandoning the house and following him. She is quite willing to find me a pair of spectacles, and offers me a grog in the bargain.

I reach the hospital.

"What am I to do with you?" asks the major. "You will simply be taken prisoner if the Germans advance. There is an evacuation train at the station. Off you go!"

This train is still almost empty: a few vans, some of which are fitted up with stretchers for the more severely wounded, and a number of third-class or second-class carriages.

I enter one of the vans: three rows of forms, two against each side, and one in the middle. Between the two sliding doors is an empty space. I lie down and watch the reinforcements, announced yesterday, pass by. The men march along gaily and in perfect order.

Desperate fighting is going on a few kilometres away. Wounded soldiers now pour into the station; they are being brought up direct from the firing line.

Ha! here comes a man of my own squadron. He is wounded in the arm. On catching sight of me, he exclaims—

"What! were you not killed?"

"No, I am still alive, you see."

"But you are reported dead. Some of the company saw you fall, hurled to the ground beneath a 210 shot."

"Is that all?"

The van fills up, but the stretcher-bearers continue to bring others.

"There is no more room here, I suppose?"

"There are already more than forty of us."

"Close up a little. We must find room for every one."

We do the best we can; I lean against the form in such a way that the sergeant seated in front of me places on it his two injured feet which have just been hurriedly dressed. It is a shell wound, and the wrappings are speedily soaked with blood.

There is a man walking to and fro the entire length of the train outside; his head is bandaged, and his arm in a sling. On being told to enter the van, he makes a violent gesture of refusal, and continues his walk along the platform. A maddening performance, though necessary to numb his terrible sufferings and enable him to retain full consciousness. And this goes on for four hours.

More stretchers, each bearing a pallid and grimy sufferer. Not a cry or scream, though occasionally some poor fellow, on being involuntarily hustled, utters a long-drawn-out "Ah!" and clenches his teeth. A quite young infantryman lies outstretched between the doors, both legs swathed in wadding. On asking how he feels, he feebly whispers, "Bien mal," and shakes his head.

Another squeeze to make room for fresh arrivals. One of these exclaims—

"What numbers of Germans have been killed! They're paying for this, I can tell you!"

From every corner exclamations are heard approving of the sentiment.

At two o'clock the train begins to move. Ever since dawn the boom of cannon has been heard without a break. A feverish sensation comes over me, and I close my eyes.

How hot it is! To obtain a little air and leave as much room as possible for the more severely wounded, I sit down by the side of a sergeant-major on the edge of the truck, my legs hanging outside the carriage.

The firs of the Vosges file past in a seemingly endless procession. At each station Red-Cross and volunteer nurses bring milk, bread and tea; frequently also cakes, eggs and preserves. Those of us who can walk serve the rest, leaving the van and returning with hands full of provisions.

At nightfall I fling myself on the floor, under a form close to the wall. Out in the open country, stoppages are frequent. From time to time the engine-driver's shrill whistles keep the way clear.

Thursday, 27th August.

The infantry sergeant has stretched his legs and placed his feet on the form under which I am lying. On awakening, I notice that the blood from his wound has been streaming over my hair and neck.

About nine o'clock we reach Gray. The men-attendants remove a few severe cases which must be operated on without delay. One part of the station has been transformed into a hospital. There are any number of majors about, and they find plenty to do.

I request permission to return to the depot; since I have no broken limbs, why should I stay on at the hospital? Accordingly I am sent to Chalindrey, where I have two hours to wait for the Langres train.

I wonder if I can find a chemist's shop. One is pointed out to me. The chemist looks me over with considerable suspicion and mistrust. A shapeless *képi*, a dirty, threadbare coat, and an unshaven face all covered with mud are not prepossessing features. He asks—

"My dear fellow, what do you do in ordinary times?"

Respect for the journal causes me to hesitate somewhat. But then, this war excuses everything, and I confess—

"I am on the editorial staff of the *Figaro*, monsieur."

"Indeed? you don't look like it!"

He laughs heartily, introduces his wife, and ... invites me to lunch.

My hosts have three sons at the front; they attend to my wants as though I were one of these. Then they motor me back to Humes. I cannot find words to thank them, nor do I know how to tell them that I will not forget their kindness.

The Hôtel Girardot and *Père Achille* at the door! He recognizes me.

"A ghost!"

Everybody comes running up.

Reymond, from the loft, thinks he hears my voice. He clambers down and stands amazed at my cadaverous appearance.

"Can it be you, dear old fellow?" he asks. "Well, well, you are a pretty sight!"

He grasps my hands; still I can find nothing to say. Then he carries me off to the lieutenant, the commander, the major.

"Is there a bed for him?" asks the latter.

"Yes."

"Well, let him have it at once, and don't let him be moved. If no complications show themselves to-morrow, he will be on his feet in three days."

They hoist me into the loft. "The Spy" has left, and so I take possession of the folding-bed. Verrier, who has come running up, tucks me in. A corporal, who knows all about drugs, briskly rubs turpentine into my skin.

"Anything fresh here?" I ask.

"I should think so. Two days after you left a new detachment was sent out, including 'the Spy,' Raoul, and Lefranc."

Lefranc was first violin at the Colonne concerts. He would sometimes come up into our loft and play Ravel and Stravinski for us. Down below in the stable slept a couple of muleteers. They shouted out—

"Haven't you nearly finished up in the loft? How do you expect us to sleep with all this squeaking overhead?"

Thereupon Lefranc played a slow drawling valse, and the muleteers calmed down.

Reymond continues—

"Roberty comes here every day now. It will soon be our turn to leave. Within a week Humes will probably see no more of us."

"Do you belong to Class 4?"

"Yes."

"Then I must make haste to get well, in which case I may accompany you."

CHAPTER III

AT THE DEPOT

Saturday, 29th August.

I am now able to rise, and, with the aid of a stick, go to all four musters of the company. I recognize the heaps of dung, the geese, ducks and cows, and the snivelling little children. My comrades in the section regard me as "the one who has seen fire."

Sunday, 30th August.

We are assured this morning that the Germans are in Amiens.

Monday, 31st August.

I go to Langres to restore my outfit, for I have nothing left. All I had so carefully prepared or bought in Paris the few days preceding my departure—foot-gear, linen, repairing materials, field-dressing, tobacco, chocolate, toilet bag and writing-paper—utterly disappeared in the Vosges on the 25th.

I take a real bath in a real bathroom, and the sensation is glorious. Former baths I had always taken in mechanical fashion, without thinking, but now I savour and relish the joy and delight of it.

The most contradictory rumours are abroad; some proclaim great victories, others a rapid advance of the Germans by the north. There is entire confidence, however.

Tuesday, 1st September.

Réveillé at three o'clock. The men who are well trained and ready to leave, and those who are weakly and more or less raw, are divided out into separate companies.

The lieutenant delivers an energetic little discourse on the subject of discipline; the new-comers, unaccustomed to being harangued by their commanders, regard him as some bloodthirsty tiger.

They murmur sadly to one another—

"What beastly luck to fall in with such a tartar!"

Useless to explain that the lieutenant is a charming fellow, and that this is only his way, the new-comers sorrowfully shake their heads.

Five hundred men are to leave to-day. Verrier is one of the number, so we make due preparations for his departure.

At seven in the evening the detachment leaves Humes. Shall we ever see Verrier again? Where is he going, and what is taking place? Reymond and I return to the hotel with downcast mien. Just one drink before climbing the ladder up into the loft. Assuredly it is sadder to stay behind than to depart.

Wednesday, 2nd September.

Whenever we are free we have interesting conversations under the apple-tree with Lieutenant Roberty. The month of September will decide the war. On the 1st of November we shall all be back home.

In the Paris journals of the 29th August we read of "the situation of our front from the Somme to the Vosges...."

The Somme! We thought this phrase was simply a local *canard*, that by a typographical error the word *Somme* had replaced the word *Sambre*. We imagined that fighting was still going on in Belgium. And the communiqué of the 30th states that the Imperial Guard received a check at Guise....

We read, without any great interest, details upon the constitution of the new ministry. No doubt the situation is serious. There is no infatuation here. We are still in quarters, with just the ordinary drill.

Thursday, 3rd September.

We muster. The 27th is drawn up for marching, so we shall not be here long.

Three from the 28th pass into our squadron: Varlet, an electrician, a short, dark fellow with a large, pointed nose and faithful, intelligent eyes; Jacquard, a little man who vainly tries to shout as loudly as Varlet, whose voice is that of a mob orator; lastly, Charensac, who comes from Auvergne, and resembles Sancho Panza in being as broad as he is tall. The latter man has a roguish little dark moustache, and a beard that covers his neck. He wears his *képi* on the back of his head, over his neck. His paunch protrudes in the same extravagant fashion. The fellow seems determined to treat the war as a huge joke. These three march in the second rank; Reymond and I in the first, along with Corporal Bernier and a Doctor of Law named Maxence.

The latter four have rather long legs, whereas Varlet, Jacquard, and Charensac have short ones.

The result is that we hear them grumbling as they march—

"Not so fast; we cannot follow you. One would think you had been feeding on gazelle's flesh!"

The tall ones take longer strides than ever. When we halt for a moment words are bandied about, and a quarrel seems imminent.

Friday, 4th September.

This morning I was able to march twenty kilometres. I have regained my old form.

Out in the streets there is talk of a possible departure for Paris. The depot may be transferred to some town in the centre of France.

We learn that the Government has left Paris for Bordeaux.... This is rather astonishing news.

When will this life in depots and barracks come to an end? When others are fighting and being killed, to mount guard by the watering-trough for the purpose of preventing soldiers from washing their socks is intolerable.

Saturday, 5th September.

No marching or drill to-day, since the order to leave may arrive any moment.

The English, says the communiqué, have taken ten cannon in the forest of Compiègne....

The Germans at Compiègne?... The train from Paris did not arrive this morning. It is becoming quite stifling here.

What is worse than the official dispatches is the multiplication of fantastic news. A famous airman has been shot as a spy; a mined forest in the neighbourhood of Lunéville has been fired, destroying three German army corps....

From Brittany a telegram reaches me dated 31st August. It has been only five days on the road!

Just now there returned to the depot with a bullet in his arm a man who left on the 23rd August, like myself. He has been a sergeant-major, belonging to Class 1886, who gave up his stripes and joined again. As I had seen him fall, I imagined he was dead. Like a couple of old soldiers, we recall the plain strewn with projectiles and all the incidents of that day on the battlefield. On the evening of the 25th he counted seventeen villages in flames.

Whilst boasting of our campaigns, Reymond, who is just behind us, recites —

Dost remember, Viscount, that half-lune we captured from the enemy at the siege of Arras?

What's that thou say'st? A half-lune indeed! It was a full lune, I tell thee....

Sunday, 6th September.

At the seven o'clock muster the quartermaster reads out the orders for the day —

"Sunday, rest and labour [*travaux*] incidental to the cleanliness of the body."

The word *travaux* will give some faint indication of the trouble needed to get the dirt out of one's skin.

Washing of clothes and a bathe in the Mouche. Eager perusal, beneath the apple-tree, of letters and journals three days old.

Endless discussion and jokes on the "considerable factor" of which Lord Kitchener can say nothing more than that it will come to the help of the Allies. At Humes the watchword is *"Cherchez le facteur!"* ("Find the postman!")

No defeat has been announced, and yet the Germans are at Senlis! No use trying to understand, as we used to say in barracks. Fighting and killing is going on whilst we are doing nothing but chatter beneath the apple-tree.

Monday, 7th September.

A comrade receives a letter from his mother telling him of the possible entry of the Germans into Paris. Most improbable; how are we to believe such a thing? And yet the terms of the letter are most distinct and detailed. By common consent we leave this subject of conversation and begin to speak of the Russian victories.

Tuesday, 8th September.

We now form part of a detachment of five hundred men with our friend Roberty in command. We shall proceed to the front either this evening or to-morrow.

This morning an engine-driver told us at the station that in the neighbourhood of Reims the French have made great hecatombs of Germans. He saw the corpses heaped up in piles. One piece of good news at all events.

I take my leave of the Girardot family; we shake hands and drink healths. Then I fondle and caress the huge dog, the *chien à sonnettes*, whose bell gives forth a more melancholy tinkle than ever.

The campaign at Humes is ended.

CHAPTER IV

EN ROUTE

Wednesday, 9th September.

The order to leave came this evening. Our detachment is to join up with the 352nd.

Final preparations: all the tins of preserves we had piled up in Girardot's loft are divided out amongst the men of the squadron; these tins—*foies gras*, tongue, knuckle of ham, corned beef—are called *Rimailhos*, because of their calibre.

At seven in the morning we leave Humes. The entire depot is present, and the people of the district bring us flowers with which we adorn our rifles. Roll-call. A short address by the commander of the depot. Shouts of "Vive la France!" *En route* as we thunder forth the *Marseillaise*.

At Langres station we pile up our rifles. A few innocent fellows scribble post-cards, whilst we poke fun at them.

"Do you mean to say you're writing? You know it will never reach its desti-nation!"

There is a sense of satisfaction, however, in sending a thought to those at home.

The train is ready. Our haversacks are strapped on and we line up on the plat-form. The regulations order silence, but each man is shouting with all his might. When the train begins to move, there are ten heads and shoulders pressing out at the windows. We again shriek out the *Marseillaise*. In point of fact, where are we going? Where is the 352nd? No one knows, not even Roberty.

He has chosen our squadron to supply a police guard for the train. This is a sign of favouritism: the police guard fills three first-class compartments, whilst the other poor fellows are piled in tens in third-class carriages, or even in vans. At each station the guard jump down on to the platform, bayonet fixed, and helmet strapped round the chin. Theoretically they must see to it that no one leaves the station. In reality they say to their comrades, who disperse in every direction—

"Fetch me a quart, old man! See, here's my can! You understand I cannot go myself as it is my business to prevent any one leaving."

Belin, our corporal, has served nine years in the Foreign Legion, and so he knows the ropes. The gentlest and pleasantest of companions. In the two first-class carriages, besides Roberty, are Reymond and myself, Maxence, whom I have already mentioned, a handsome fellow from the Franche-Comté, head taller than the rest of us, a lawyer and big landed proprietor, who knows Verlaine by heart, and lastly, Jacquard, Varlet and Charensac.

The day is spent in eating preserved food, smoking pipes, playing cards, and roaring out songs and jokes.

Sometimes the train stops for a couple of hours in the open country. Men go off into the fields for the sheer pleasure of disobeying orders and stretching their limbs; when they see the train once again on the move they come running up like madmen and soon overtake it, for the driver carries us along at a jog-trot pace.

A comic alarm during the night: sudden firing in the neighbourhood of Troyes. Is the train being attacked, in the way we read about in a schoolboy's romance? Our valiant men, leaping up from sleep, immediately cram cartridges in their rifles and jump out on to the track. Simply a few petards exploded on the rails. Now we can sleep.

Thursday, 10th September.

Corbeil. Six hours' forced inactivity! We make some coffee along the track. A train full of wounded enters the station. We hurry to the doors of the vans and find that they are packed with soldiers of all sorts, lying *pêle-mêle* on the floor, arms, legs and heads intertwined. The uniforms are unrecognizable and in rags, covered with dust and blood.

And we, who are proceeding to the firing line, gaze open-mouthed on those who have just come back from it. Evidently there is terrible fighting going on, but the wounded have little to say. With a shake of the head they remark—

"Yes, yes, things are progressing ... but it's a tough business!"

"We are winning, are we not?"

"Yes, but it takes time!"

Bayonet charges, frightful whirling gusts of shot and shell, fields and woods strewn with dead, the moaning of the wounded; such is a summary of what each man has witnessed, just a tiny corner of the battle. No clear general impression. Unshaken confidence in the final result, along with a consciousness of the difficulty of the task.

A carriage filled with German prisoners. We elbow one another to catch a glimpse of them. One of them, his shoulder and arm all twisted up, asks—

"Are you reservists?"

Some one nods assent.

Thereupon he says—

"I, too, am a reservist like you."

Anxious to create a feeling of sympathy, he exhibits his wound.

I say to him—

"*Mon garçon*, you shouldn't have gone to war."

No sooner has one train left the station than another steams up; for several hours the wounded file past without a break.

At five in the evening the lieutenant, after a long conversation with the station-master, announces that the detachment is to cross Paris. Delirious joy.

We reach the Gare de Lyons and, shouldering arms, proceed in columns of fours to the Gare Saint-Lazare.

Our men hail every taxi-cab driver they see.

"I say, old man, just go and tell my wife ... or my mother ... or my sister, will you? She lives in such a street, such a number. Hurry up and bring her along."

"All right!"

Off goes the chauffeur. Half an hour after he is back with the whole family, and, amid the emotion and excitement of so unexpected a reunion, slips away without a thought of payment.

Halt in front of the Cirque d'Hiver. We pile our rifles and take off our haversacks. The crowd collects around and proves very emotional. Useless to say to one's friends or relatives—

"Don't carry things too far, we are not coming back, we are only going!"

The good-natured public will listen to nothing; they give us credit and treat us as heroes just the same.

A second halt at Rue Auber. The crowd around grows larger and larger. It appears that Paris has been really threatened. This morning's communiqué, however, states that the enemy has retired a distance of forty kilometres.

At the Gare Saint-Lazare more than two hundred out of the five hundred men belonging to the detachment have their family around them.

At nine the train is waiting and we have to leave. We embrace and shout, laugh and cry, promise to return soon and to write.

Roberty, Reymond and I have made up our mind to travel first-class. In one of the compartments a very stylish, gentlemanly-looking individual has installed himself. Strapping my helmet under my chin, I assume a tone of voice at once firm and courteous, and say—

"I beg pardon, monsieur, but you are occupying a seat reserved for the chief."

The gentleman, abashed, vaguely stammers some excuse or other, hurriedly snatches up his valise and travelling rug and looks for another seat.

When he has gone, I remark—

"What a bouncer!"

The three of us sprawl at our ease over the six seats, posing as well-to-do persons off on a holiday.

We walk along the passage. A wounded corporal, belonging to Class 12, promises us victory, and is intoxicated at the prospect.

In reply to our questions, he says—

"You ask if we have got them? We're simply sweeping the ground with them! I killed one this afternoon, a sergeant. Here's his shoulder tab and his belt clasp. Read the words on it: *Gott mit uns*. What brazen effrontery!

"Just think, he was running away. I caught him up and gave him a dig with my bayonet between the shoulders. Then, do you know what the cur did? He actually turned round and wounded me. I gave him another thrust and finished him off.

"I could never have thought it would give one so jolly a feeling to kill a man."

After a moment's reflection—

"After all, this is an ugly cut in the thigh. He might have maimed me for life."

"That's perhaps what he wanted to do."

The wounded man sinks into a meditative mood. All through the night we roll along until we reach our station, when we descend and march away for the front.

Friday, 11th September.

About noon we enter the devastated zone at Dammartin: the telegraph lines have been torn down. Right and left of the road trees lie stretched on the ground; heaps of ashes are all that remains of the hayricks. In a ditch lies a corpse in red trousers and blue coat. Most of the men of the detachment have not yet been in the fighting line, and this is the first dead man, left lying on the ground, that they have seen. They are considerably moved, and even surprised.

We reach Nanteuil-le-Haudouin. The station has been destroyed. A convoy of provisions and supplies passes, escorted by cuirassiers. A glorious sunset.

A prolonged halt in front of the *mairie*. The place is full of troops and the mayor is at loss where to put us up.

"Go to Wattebled's farm," he says to the lieutenant.

This is a fine farm, though situated at the farther end of the town. The farmer is serving. Officers of the enemy have lodged in the building and have left the place in a dreadful condition. All the cupboards and wardrobes have been ransacked, and the contents flung about the rooms. The cellar is empty; broken bottles lie in every corner.

The beds, however, have been left intact. We quickly stretch ourselves at full length, delighted to rest after travelling for two nights and three days. The dinner has been nothing to boast of—neither bread nor wine, and scarcely any light.

Saturday, 12th September.

Whilst awaiting fresh supplies, which postpone our departure several hours, we explore the district. Those stores whose proprietors were absent have been methodically pillaged; whatever could not be carried away has been broken to pieces. In the wine and tobacco shops nothing but the walls are left standing.

On the doors, chalk inscriptions indicate which German troops were quartered there. The inhabitants are still somewhat scared; they can hardly believe in their good fortune at finding themselves safe.

We obtain as much rum and wine as we want from a wholesale wine dealer! The Germans had had time neither to remove nor to destroy his barrels and hogsheads. The news spreads like wildfire through the quarters.

Each squadron delegates a man laden with cans slung over his shoulder. They press around the barrels in an endless file. An artillery officer wishes to prevent the infantry from approaching the wine store, especially his own men. Howls and protests. Lieutenant Roberty has to intervene before we can enter the place.

Meanwhile, the stores have arrived. Whilst the pots are boiling we improvise a lunch for twenty-five in the large dining-room. The manager lends us napkins and a tablecloth, plates and glasses, and even a *jardinière* for putting flowers on the table. Our ordinary fare includes a fillet of beef and we have bought three fowls. Each man brings his own wine and bread.

This sybaritic life, however, cannot last indefinitely. At two o'clock we make our way through a district which has witnessed terrible battles. Arms and equipments, *képis* and helmets and cloaks strew the ground. The smell of decomposing bodies passes in whiffs; it proceeds mainly from dead horses, still unburied, rotting away, their bodies all swollen and their legs rigid. By the side of a stack of hay three German corpses await the services of a grave-digger. Their greyish-green uniform seems to harmonize with the colour of the hay.

At the halt, in a carriage left behind by the enemy, we find Berlin journals telling of victories in Belgium, along with a confused mass of note-books, nightlights—very convenient articles, these,—a broken phonograph, and German postcards all containing wishes that the recipients may have a good time in Paris, etc.

Peasants come along with tales that uhlans are lurking in the neighbourhood. We waste a couple of hours in sending patrols to scour the woods. Not a single uhlan to be seen. We are caught in a shower of rain and reach Lévignen at nightfall, wet through. The silence and solitude are intense. Enormous gaps in the houses have been made by shells. The gamekeeper—perhaps the only inhabitant—proposes to the lieutenant that the detachment be lodged in the church. By the light of candles which are speedily lit, the men make the best of the situation, only too pleased to be out of the rain. The church, however, is too small. Half the detachment wanders about the abandoned village as the downpour continues.

At all hazards we enter a house. No one is there, but we find beds, a stove and wood. There is no water, however, for making coffee, so I fill a large bowl with the rain streaming from a spout. A few tins of preserved meat and some wine have been left behind, so the lieutenant, Belin, Reymond, Maxence and myself easily manage to make a good meal and to sleep under a sheltering roof.

Sunday, 13th September.

It appears that there is a dead German at the *mairie*. We go to look at him. There the fellow lies, stretched on the floor. His head is concealed beneath his arms; his sides, back and legs have been stripped bare by a shell explosion and he has evidently dragged himself here to die. A smell of decomposing flesh puts us to flight.

The detachment again starts off early across a devastated land. We are gaily received by the inhabitants of Villers-Cotterets, who, delivered from the enemy a couple of nights previously, fête the French troops incessantly marching into the town.

We quarter ourselves in the goods station, already partly occupied by wounded soldiers awaiting evacuation. Two Red Cross ladies, who had remained during the occupation, are kept busily employed. One of them appears behind a huge pot filled with coffee, from which the wounded help themselves. A German, his field-grey uniform in tatters, his jaws contracted and arms and legs all twisted up, is dying in a corner between two men attendants who do their best to relieve his agony. Other Germans, more or less wounded, lie *pêle-mêle* on the straw near our own men. No disputes or quarrels, victors and vanquished are alike exhausted.

The town gives more than ever the impression of a grand review. This is the headquarters of the Sixth Army; motor-cars rush up and down; in the streets are soldiers of every description, staff officers, generals. A 40-h.p. motor-car, flying the Stars and Stripes, stops in front of the *mairie*: immediately we imagine that the United States ambassador has come to offer peace on behalf of Germany, and we discuss the terms and conditions we must lay down.

Flanked by gendarmes, a knot of prisoners files past. They are in rags, covered with dust, and appear worn out. Soldiers and civilians line the road and watch them intently; not an exclamation is uttered; on every face is a look of radiant gaiety, forming a striking contrast with the surly expressions of the beaten Germans. Some of the latter have humble-looking, sensitive, fresh-complexioned countenances; these are the ones who must have committed the worst atrocities of all.

We profit by the general confusion and good humour to slip into a hotel reserved for officers and indulge in a luxurious repast.

It is also by dint of cunning and astuteness that Reymond, Maxence and myself manage to find lodging with some honest people who place at our disposal two bedrooms and a dressing-room. Only the previous week they had boarded a Prussian colonel who daily explained the mathematical reasons which would ensure the triumph of Germany. And then, only two days ago, he galloped off without finishing his demonstration. He was so hurried that he kicked down his bedroom door. He was daily in the habit of locking it himself, but in his excitement he had forgotten where he had put the key ... perhaps even where the lock was! My host points to the broken panels, quite pleased to have such a proof of German disorder and confusion.

Monday, 14th September.

When shall we see white bed-sheets again? Such luxury has turned our heads, and Villers-Cotterets, intact and full of life, in the midst of a scene of ruin and desolation, seems to us the very capital of the world! The dull growl of the cannon is heard away in the distance.

An abundant supply of fresh meat, preserves and wine. *En route* for the head-quarters of the Army Corps, where directions will be given us for joining the regiment.

A long march through the forest. More dead horses and that intolerable stench of decomposing flesh which strikes one brutally full in the face like a lash.

The roar of cannon draws nearer. We halt in a field. A detachment of prisoners passes along the road.

Still the wounded come; in groups of twos, threes and fours they make their way, after a summary dressing of their wounds, in the direction of the ambulance, hobbling along, leaning on sticks or on a comrade's shoulder.

They ask—

"Is it far to Villers-Cotterets?"

"Fifteen kilometres."

"*Ah! Là là!*"

Amongst them are men of the 352nd. Having met at the depot we recognize one another, and ask—

"Are the enemy retreating?"

"No, it seems as though they were determined to halt by the river."

We also learn that shells are beginning to fall a few hundred yards distant.

At the entrance to Ambleny, near the Aisne, a staff captain stops Roberty: it is impossible to cross the bridge in the daytime; the headquarters have been transferred to Vic-sur-Aisne, which place it is too late to reach to-day. We are quartered in an abandoned saw-mill.

Our last *Rimailhos* supply us with a solid meal. There comes a knock at the door—a lost soldier in search of food and lodging. We invite him in. On seeing our repast, a broad smile illumines his face, and he remarks—

"How lucky I fell in with you!"

As the lieutenant gives him a copious portion and pours out a generous bumper of wine, the man says, his mouth full of food—

"*Merci*, Monsieur Roberty."

"What! Do you know me?"

"A little. And you also (indicating myself). I am a waiter in Lavenue's restaurant. I served you at lunch the day following the mobilization."

Greatly moved, we grasp his hand effusively, and say—

"Excuse us, old man, we did not recognize you."

He quite understands, whereupon Roberty adds—

"Now just remain seated; I'm going to serve you myself."

Dinner over, we offer him the corner containing the most abundant supply of straw, and fall off to sleep.

Tuesday, 15th September.

A long detour to reach Vic-sur-Aisne. Halt in front of the keep by the castle moat. The lieutenant goes for orders to the staff at headquarters. Whilst awaiting his return we watch German prisoners as they come and go in the enclosure.

A hostile aeroplane is hovering above the town. Received with a brisk fusillade and exploding shrapnel, it disappears. The general in command of the corps passes by on horseback, followed by a numerous staff. Lined up, behind our piles of arms, we salute. A fine subject for an Academy picture.

Roberty returns; the regiment is in the first line, between Fontenoy and Port-Fontenoy. *En route* to join it.

We proceed along the Aisne in Indian file over a bombarded road. On our left, behind the hill, fighting is taking place; always the same sound, as of carpets being beaten or planks being nailed down. Here comes a battalion of our regiment; the other is in the trenches. A bivouac is installed on the side of a hillock in a meadow surrounded by trees. Evening descends. We build huts made of trusses of straw, torn from a neighbouring stack. The stack melts away and finally disappears, having been transformed into a little negro village. The fire needed for the cooking of our meal sets up great flares of light, ... too great, in all probability, for a hail of bullets whistles about our ears. Where does it come from? Mystery!

"Put out the fires and lie flat on the ground!" shout the officers.

The bullets continue; some strike the ground with a sharp, cracking sound, others ricochet and glance off! *Piou! Piou!*

I lie there and wait until this storm of iron, more irritating than dangerous, has passed. The thought enters my mind —

"How bothering! It has even lost the attraction of novelty for me now."

As one who has already seen fire, I feel impelled to address a few words to my neighbours, Maxence and Sergeant Chaboy. Curious to gather their impressions, I crawl up to them and slyly ask —

"Well, raw ones, what do you think of the stew?"

They are both asleep. As I receive nothing but a snore for an answer, I do not insist.

Firing ceases as suddenly as it began. We rise to our feet; one man is wounded and a *gamelle* shot through. That's all.

After fire comes water; an implacable shower beats down upon our poor straw shelters, penetrating right through and laying them flat on the ground. The place must be left.

At the foot of the hill, the village of Port-Fontenoy. Every house is full of troops. Not the tiniest shed or loft is available. And here stands the colonel, buried beneath his hood, his face lit up by the intermittent lights coming from his pipe.

"Those who have just come from the depot," he says, "had better make shift in the yard here."

We make shift.

Reymond and Roberty slip away under a cart; I follow suit. Two others join us. Here, at all events, we are somewhat sheltered from the rain. I feel the ground: it is a bed of dung, and soft to the touch. Somebody's muddy shoe is pressed against my face; my back is being used as a pillow by the lieutenant. Huddling together, we feel the cold less. We have had no dinner, merely some *pâté de foie gras* spread between biscuits as hard as wood. There is a strange odour about our hands, and the dining-room is anything but comfortable.

Wednesday, 16th September.

The night has been a long one, rain falling all the time. We burst out laughing when we discover how dirty we look.

The order comes to cross the wood and reach the crest of the hill, beyond which something is happening—something serious, to judge by the noise. On the other bank of the Aisne, scarcely a kilometre distant, the small station of Ambleny-Fontenoy is being bombarded. The volleys pass over our heads, making a noise like that of a tram skidding over the rails. A flaky patch of white smoke indicates where the explosion takes place.

We make wagers as to where the next shell will fall.

That one—looking in the air to see the snorting projectile pass—will be for the station.

Pan! The red roof crumbles in. At that moment a train enters the station. The Germans see it; a projectile falls twenty yards in front of the engine; another, ten yards in front; a third, well aimed, but a little short. The engine-driver does not lose his head; he reverses the engine. Four consecutive explosions on the very spot the locomotive has just left.

Applause and shrieks of joy.

Both train and station seem very much like Nuremberg toys. One must reflect if emotion is to be genuine.

The sun's rays speedily dry our coats on our backs. Some of the men sleep, whilst the artillery duel redoubles in intensity.

Varlet has gone into the village to make lunch. He returns, furious, with dishevelled hair and empty hands.

"Well! Where's lunch?"

Varlet vociferates—

"Lunch, indeed, *Zut!* You'll have to tighten your belts a little more. A *marmite* fell right in the middle of it all."

Varlet tells his tale: he heard the whistling sound, and knew that he was in for it. He had just time to plunge head first into a dog's kennel.

"When the thing exploded," explains our cook, "there was only my head inside, the dog prevented me from entering farther."

Good-bye to lunch and the toothsome dishes. Belin is exasperated.

"How will my squadron manage for meals now?" he wonders.

Prowling about, we discover a little grotto, a comfortable shelter in case of bombardment. Meanwhile, each man makes his own conjectures. Shall we attack this evening or to-morrow? Manifestly we have not been brought here to take an afternoon nap in the sun.

Suddenly an order comes that we are to be quartered at Port-Fontenoy. The deuce! This is the point of impact, the magnet that draws all the shells of the district.

A barn full of hay and straw. We fling ourselves on to the ground and sleep comes instantaneously.

About two in the morning Jacquard, whose turn it is to stand sentry before the door, shakes Roberty, who is soundly sleeping.

"*Mon lieutenant*, shells are falling in the yard, we shall all be blown to pieces if we stay here!"

Roberty, whose capacity for sleep is quite out of the common, turns over on to his side and growls —

"All right! don't disturb me. To-morrow I will look into the matter."

Jacquard, offended, returns to his post.

Thursday, 17th September.

Standing on a slight eminence, we watch the shells, from early dawn, falling on to the station.

In the evening we return to Port-Fontenoy. This time the squadron lodges in a goat-shed. It is very warm and intimate.

Friday, 18th September.

The 6th battalion comes down from the outposts. What a state they are in! They have just spent four days and nights in the first line, in trenches improvised and devoid of shelter. And yet *we* thought ourselves dirty!

They look haggard and dazed, and are covered with mud from head to foot. We crowd around. Their first words are —

"Have you any tobacco? All ours is finished."

We supply them with tobacco, even with a superior brand of cigarette.

Thereupon interest in life returns, and they consent to talk.

"And what of Verrier? Is he alive?"

"Yes."

"Which company?"

"The 23rd."

Reymond and I run off in the direction indicated.

In front of a grotto some men are lying on the ground.

"Is this the 23rd?"

"It is."

"Is there any one here named Verrier?"

Then Verrier himself, pale, emaciated and in rags, rises from the grotto, like Lazarus from the tomb. A Mephistophelean goat-beard, which he has grown, makes his long face appear longer than ever. He sees us holding out our hands to him, but he bursts out, without the slightest greeting—

"Tell me, a war like this can't last a fortnight longer, surely, can it?"

This question puts us into a jovial mood.

"The war, old fellow? It will last a couple of years," we assure him.

"Well, then," sighs Verrier, "let me sit down."

We carry him off to Lieutenant Roberty. Then we place him in the sunshine, bring him coffee and tobacco, and lend him a brush. He feels better.

This evening the men of our detachment are distributed out amongst the various companies. The whole of our squadron becomes the first squadron of the 24th. Roberty is in command of the first section. He obtains permission for Verrier to be transferred from the 23rd to the 24th. How fortunate to be shoulder to shoulder again! It is so much easier to fight with one's friends by one's side.

CHAPTER V

A BACKWARD GLANCE—THE BATTLE OF THE MARNE

This evening, in the goat-stable, Verrier shows us his coat, pierced by seven shrapnel holes. Two of the rents are repeated in the seat of his trousers. There is a hole in his pants; the shrapnel discreetly proceeding no farther.

"I've had a rough time of it," affirms Verrier.

"Tell us what you've been doing."

Verrier, however, is no prattler.

"I will read from my note-book," he says; "that will not take so long." And he begins—

"Left Langres September 1st, nine in the evening. After sixteen hours in the train, reached Noisy-le-Sec on the 2nd. The station is filled with wounded from the north. Some moan and lament, others, with half-closed eyes, seem on the point of death. All have enormous dressings, stained with blood. Nurses eagerly attend to their needs.

On the platforms, *pêle-mêle* with the soldiers, stand groups of families, refugees from Belgium, the Ardennes and the Aisne. Women, seated on enormous bundles, weep all the time, though they keep an eye on the urchins as the latter play with the soldiers.

At Argenteuil-Triage we cross a train of English infantry: open, clean-shaven, boyish faces, laughing heartily. They are in spick and span condition. We shout greetings to one another. In the distance I perceive the Eiffel Tower, which seems to me the finest monument in the world. At Argenteuil, Archères, and all the stations, stand women, children, and old men along the line, cheering us as we pass, and sending kisses after us.

On the night of the 3rd we are still *en route*. The lines are blocked, causing detours and occasioning delays. At Mantes we learn that the German cavalry have put in an appearance at Compiègne and Senlis. We are informed that the Government is leaving for Bordeaux. We descend at Bourget, and at Chennevières-les-Louvres rejoin the regiment, which has been put to a severe trial at Proyart, in the Somme. It is then sent to the rear and entrusted with the duty of protecting the retreat. I am transferred to the 23rd company.

On the 4th we take up our quarters at Moussy, Seine-et-Marne. The army headquarters have been set up here. Not a single inhabitant; shops all closed and houses abandoned. Impossible to procure anything, even by offering gold. On the other hand, there is considerable military animation; troops file past on their way to take up new positions.

On the 6th of September we are up at one in the morning and depart at two. The road is obstructed: an artillery regiment, teams of pontooners, stretcher-bearers, a supply train. The cannon is rumbling in the north. We have the impression of being at drill; the same gaiety and *insouciance*. We think of nothing but singing, eating, and drinking.

Arrival at Dammartin, where scarcely a hundred out of fifteen hundred inhabitants are left.

At noon, *en route* in the direction of Meaux, across ploughed land. A scorching sun.

Only at six in the evening does the regiment form in battle line. The two battalions, under the protection of strong patrols, form a solid front; the companies in sections, four in a line, at a distance of fifty paces. The officers have left their mounts. The advance is very slow; not a word is said. The cannon make a deafening din. Numerous stacks of straw are aflame.

Night comes on. The order is given to fling away our cigarettes. Shortly afterwards: Supplies ready! Fix bayonets!

On the horizon, light appears all around.

The regiment reaches the border of a village which, after a violent fight, has just been retaken from the enemy. Ours the mission to keep it at all costs.

Supper at ten. We sleep in the open air.

We are up at four in the morning of the 7th of September. The German artillery opens a violent fire on the village, which we cross at a run, bent double, Indian file, keeping close to the walls. Not one of us is wounded. We come down into a ravine, above which hover a couple of Taubes. At no great height they pass to and fro, without appearing to suffer from the violent fusillade directed against them. They are trying to find the very batteries in aid of which my section has been sent out.

The shells begin to rain down upon us in uninterrupted streams. We rush into a wood skirting the ravine. We form a carapace. Two hours on the ground, without stirring, crouching up against one another, our haversacks over our heads. Each explosion covers us with dust and hot smoke. Stones, clods of earth, branches of trees fall on our backs and set our *gamelles* clanging. The company loses five dead and a score wounded. Corporal Marcelin has his head torn off by my side. During a pause we lunch. At one o'clock the performance recommences. Again a carapace is formed. An artillery officer shouts to us as he passes—

'You are in a very dangerous zone.'

No doubt of that!

This evening we bivouac out in the open.

The 8th of September, *en route* at four in the morning. We are massed in reserve behind stacks of straw, where we see something of the battle. The Germans appear to have the advantage. Their guns shower upon us huge projectiles which, on bursting, release a heavy black smoke. Violent replies by our 75's. A village to our right is aflame. Gusts of artillery fire on Fosse-Martin and the farm of Nogeon. Conflagrations are seen on all sides. An ambulance is girdled with flames.

General Joffre's order of the day is read aloud by a sergeant: 'Die rather than retreat.' The impression it leaves is profound. The paper passes from hand to hand, each man peruses it in silence. We are given a few explanations on the battle being fought, and the arrival of the 4th Corps is announced. In effect, we soon see a number of regiments advancing.

In the afternoon, an endless stream of wounded, coming for the most part from the village which has been burning ever since morning. Fighting is going on from house to house. Some of the men have terrible wounds, still undressed, from which the blood is streaming. A dragoon, who remains on horseback, has his left foot blown away, with the exception of the heel, which still hangs to the leg. An infantryman, his shoulder almost torn from his body, has abandoned his coat and converted his shirt into a sling to support his arm.

The village on the right has had to be evacuated by our troops. We must recapture it. The 5th battalion of the regiment is retiring, with standard unfurled, the 18th and 20th companies, in front, forming two successive lines of skirmishers; the 17th and 19th a short distance behind. Anxiously we watch them leave. At six o'clock the battalion returns, having made good the loss. The village has been retaken without a struggle, the Germans, driven back in other quarters, having had to abandon it.

We spend the night in a barn at Fosse-Martin. Distribution of provisions and tobacco. We make ourselves some coffee. Close by is an ambulance: broad streams of blood flow from it on to the road. The stretcher-bearers set out with dark lanterns in search of the wounded.

One o'clock in the morning, bustle and confusion. A sentry calls out: 'To arms!' Everybody rushes out with fixed bayonets. A false alarm, it was only a fire: a stack of hay aflame about two hundred yards away. The company spends the rest of the night in a neighbouring field of corn, but there is no more sleep for me.

On the following day the 23rd is appointed to support the artillery. This time we dig trenches. These we cover over with straw and beetroot leaves; and whenever a hostile aeroplane is signalled we disappear. Everybody laughs and jokes. Games of cards are started down in our holes. We have ravenous appetites.

The firing sounds farther away. There is a rumour that the enemy is retiring.

We remain where we are until the following afternoon, the 10th September. Everything is perfectly quiet. After a gay lunch we stroll about a little. We notice French aeroplanes returning to headquarters at Brégy.

In the evening we are quartered at Bouillancy, abandoned on the 7th by the Germans after a severe struggle: roofs and walls knocked in, windows and blinds broken and torn down. A few houses are still burning, but all the inhabitants have fled. I try to start a conversation with an old fellow and his wife who are obstinately bent on remaining behind and have lived here several days, hiding in their cellar. They are quite stupefied with the recent events, and it is impossible to obtain any information from them.

Out in the fields stretcher-bearers are picking up the French and German wounded; in many cases gangrene has set in, as they have been lying there for five days unattended.

On the morrow we start again and cross a corner of the battlefield. In the trenches lie piles of German corpses. The French dead—all belonging to the 4th— have their faces covered with a white cloth. Bands of territorials pour petrol over the dead horses and set fire to them; they exhale a pestilential odour.

Rain begins to fall and the dust is converted into mud. The regiment reaches Villers-Cotterets by way of the forest. There are manifest proofs that the German retreat has been a very disorderly one. The ground is strewn with rifles and loaders, outfits, yellow haversacks, and broken bicycles.

A few of the inhabitants have already returned to the villages. They are beginning to become more reassured, but they are very hungry. The Germans have emptied the cellars and carried off everything eatable.

At ten in the evening we reach Villers-Cotterets, which the enemy occupied for eleven days, and from which he fled this very morning at half-past nine. At eleven our light cavalry entered. The damage is insignificant.

We leave Villers-Cotterets on the morning of the 12th. At the exit of the town the road is strewn for three or four kilometres with the most diverse objects, mainly broken bottles.

We halt at Cœuvres. A convoy of prisoners. They scarcely utter a word, remain aloof, and seem contented with their lot. They are ignorant of the fact that England is at war with Germany.

On Sunday, the 13th, we return to the danger zone. On both sides the cannon is thundering away. North and south, east and west, hayricks and farms are aflame. The regiment quarters at Ressons-le-Long.

On the 14th, at four in the morning, alarm. We cross the Aisne on a bridge of boats, near Fontenoy. The church steeple threatens ruin if it falls. We climb a steep hill; the ground is strewn with the dead bodies of French and Germans. Last night a terrible hand-to-hand fight with bayonets took place here, and the road is dotted with pools of blood. Many of the bodies have remained in the position in which they received the death-blow: an officer is kneeling on the ground in the attitude of reloading his rifle. His complexion is waxen, his eyes glazed, and his mouth open. Another lies stretched full length across the path, his arms outspread in the form of a cross. We have to stride over the body.

On the top of the hill the company deploys along a footpath in skirmish line. We now discover that the enemy is less than four hundred yards distant. A German battery pours in a raking storm of shells. No holes anywhere about, not the slightest hillock behind which to shelter. I am hurled into the air and fall back on the same spot. Wounded men shriek for help or die in agonies of convulsion; others run to the ambulance. The man by my side is shot dead; from his skull flows a stream of blood which gradually covers the whole of his face. I remove his haversack and use it to protect my own head. Then I fall asleep. When I awake I find that I am surrounded with dead bodies. The few survivors lie there absolutely motionless, for no sooner does a head rise than a bullet hisses past and artillery firing recommences. I pretend to be dead.

At five in the evening, what remains of the company crawls away in the direction of a little wood, a few hundred yards in the rear. For a whole hour, in the darkness of the night, I hear a wounded man moan piteously: '*Maman! Maman!*'

During the 15th, 16th, and 17th, we are favoured by the uncertain shelter of the wood. The rain is pouring down in torrents. The cannonade and rifle fire continue without interruption. A few more men are wounded. On the evening of the 17th, the relief is effected to the accompaniment of a hail of bullets."

Verrier has finished his reading.

CHAPTER VI

BEFORE FONTENOY

Saturday, 19th September.

The regiment is appointed to be an Army Corps reserve. We cross the Aisne early in the morning and prepare support trenches three kilometres in the rear. This is the first time we play at digging holes in the ground. It appears that the Germans dig them, and that they prove useful. Navvies' picks and shovels are distributed. We work in twos; one digging hard and the other clearing away the earth whilst the first man is resting. By the end of the day the section has dug up a trench deep enough for one to walk in without being seen.

This evening we are quartered at Ressons-le-Long, in an old round tower, of venerable aspect, adjoining a farm.

The regiment has left the east and proceeded northwards, before coming down in the direction of Paris. Then it took part in the battle of the Marne, and finally stopped on the banks of the Aisne. Still no letters!

The battalion claims the services of a postman, a busy, anxious-looking man. From time to time he stops and opens his bags in some quiet corner and blurts out about a hundred names, which he reads from envelopes chosen indiscriminately. A few of the men are there.

Sometimes there is a Dubois who answers: "Present."

The postman looks up sternly.

"Dubois what. What's your other name?"

"Dubois, Charles."

With a scornful shrug of the shoulders—

"The letter I have here is for Dubois, Emile. Why do you make me lose my time?"

The same thing happens with the Duponts, the Durands, and the Martins. The one present never possesses the right Christian name.

The postman throws back the letters into his big bag and continues his round.

"They're always asking for letters," he grumbles, "but when I bring any they never come for them."

"They" frequently have a good reason for not coming, they may well have met their death between two posts.

The postman finds his bags swelling in bulk a little more every day; he becomes more anxious and careworn than ever.

Sinister rumours are spread regarding his intentions.

"He says that if the men are not there when he calls out the names to-morrow, he will burn everything left in the bag."

"The deuce! But did he mention where the distribution was to take place?"

He has done nothing of the kind; the hour and place of distribution are the postman's secret.

Sunday, 20th September.

We are up at three in the morning. The guns begin to boom. Gradually day appears. Returning to our trenches we see flashes leaping from the cannons' mouth along with tiny puffs of smoke.

The view extends over the valley of the Aisne. The Germans are making desperate efforts to cross the river.

From our position in reserve we watch cyclists rushing along the road. The colonel comes and goes, and gives orders, smoking his huge pipe the while. A telephone has been fitted up in a haystack, from which he does not wander far, as the tinkling call is continually being heard. It is raining. We cover our trenches with sheaves of straw gathered from the neighbouring field and await events, crouching deep in our holes.

Roberty keeps us posted in what is taking place. Being a lieutenant, he is privileged to apply for the latest information from the colonel. At two o'clock the enemy takes Fontenoy, and his vanguard has descended right to the bridge of boats. He is stopped short by a company of engineers. The Germans are decimated by a well-directed fire; those who are not killed return in disorder. Our regiment is charged with the task of recapturing Fontenoy.

We fix our haversacks, take in a supply of provisions and *en route*. The descent into the valley is through a wood. Roberty roguishly declares—

"Boys, our chances of death have gone up ninety per cent."

Halt at a crossing, near the Aisne, as we await the order to attack. We place our haversacks on the ground, rest our rifles against them and sit down. An hour passes. Two batteries of 75's are firing away behind us without a pause. The rain continues.

The lieutenant is summoned to the colonel. He returns with a smile and announces—

"Our chances of death are down; Fontenoy has been recaptured without our help. The artillery have compelled the Germans to evacuate. We shall spend the night at Gorgny."

Monday, 21st; Tuesday, 22nd; and Wednesday, 23rd September.

Three days well occupied. We are quartered in a wretched-looking farm, reeking with manure and filth of every kind.

We rise at a quarter to three. It is quite cold. We hurry to the kitchen, where Varlet and Charensac, the cooks of our section, are preparing coffee and cooking beefsteaks. They have not slept at all; in fact, they only received supplies about ten at night, for revictualment carts can approach the line only in the dark. The fire flames up in the vast country chimney, lighting up the whole room. The farmer and his wife, grumbling and blink-eyed, are seated in a corner.

The coffee is very hot; already we feel better. It is followed by a quart of broth. Then Varlet portions out to each man a small piece of calcined meat: the beefsteak for the noon meal. *En route.* And now begins what Reymond calls the "noble game of the beetroot field."

I am fully convinced that in times of peace beetroots are extremely useful. This year, however, they poison the very existence of the foot-soldier, already sufficiently embittered. Ploughing one's way through fields of beetroots is enough to make one hate the war. Your foot twists and slips about in all directions. Hurled forward, you bruise your nose against the haversack of the man in front. Pulled backward, you receive from the man behind a blow in your ribs with the butt-end of his rifle. The night air is filled with groans and complaints. Where are we going? How can the officers find their way in the dark? One after another, feeling our way, each man runs in the wake of a fugitive shadow. On reaching the edge of the wood, we lose the path. The column is broken. Which direction are we to take? The wrong one, of course. Then heart-breaking rushes to and fro; we find every company except our own. Finally, day appears.

Arrival at the trenches. Distribution of shovels and picks, and quick—to work. A very pleasant form of exercise: if it is raining you wallow about in mud; if it is dry you swallow sand all the time.

Close by us belch forth our 75's, which the Germans would fain dislodge. Gradually the enemy's artillery riddles the entire plain with shot of every calibre.

Nothing lessens that noisy good-humour peculiar to ourselves. The only thing that troubles us is with reference to eating and drinking. At such times as these, this is no easy problem to solve in the case of persons endowed with a good appetite. Only a few days ago we had scruples about cleanliness, and seized every opportunity of washing ourselves. Now we never think of it. It takes an effort to imagine what life must have been like in the good old times of peace and civilization—forty days ago!

I have not had my shoes off since we left Villers-Cotterets.

Roberty dispatches Jules, his orderly, to hunt about for something fit to eat. Off goes Jules; he is a man of poaching instincts, and being of seductive manners, receives unlimited credit. Along difficult paths, known to none but himself, he reaches Ambleny, or Ressons, or Gorgny. After several hours' absence he returns in triumph, bringing a large pot filled with an abominable cold stew which the squadron tastes.

"It is made of a rabbit and an old hen," he explains. "I had them cooked together, along with some potatoes to make it more consistent."

In a huge *musette*, Jules has also brought some white bread just baked, a number of pears, two pots of preserves, and a few bottles of wine. "This is good cheer!" we say.

And so the day passes. If there is nothing to do we carve fantastic animals out of beetroots: one way of obtaining our revenge on that odious vegetable.

At twilight we give up our picks and shovels and go down towards the village. A second edition of the noble game of the beetroot field.

It is nine o'clock before we reach the farm. We receive our provision supplies, have them cooked, and eat our supper; it is nearly midnight before we are asleep. And we have to be up before three in the morning!

During the night of the 23rd, Roberty awakes us to give news of the war. In the first place—and this explains the French retreat after Charleroi—the enemy attacked us with no fewer than thirty-three corps. Then again, it appears that the Germans have recaptured oriental Prussia.... Consequently, we cannot trust too confidently in the Russian steam-roller.

We drop off to sleep again.

Thursday, 24th September.

The regiment crosses the Aisne along the bridge of boats, and passes through Port-Fontenoy, which the recent bombardments have severely tested. Those killed last Sunday have been removed by our engineers. Our goat stable is in ruins. It was indeed time for us to remove.

We reach a ravine close to the first line. The cannonade is more violent than ever.

The most recent news brought by the cooks state that Generals Castelnau and Maunoury, to be precise, have decided on a general offensive. The regiment is to take part in it.

What kind of special wire is it that connects a kitchen with headquarters? It is round the fires on which dinner is being cooked that we receive the most minute information regarding the slightest intentions of the heads of the army. This is due not only to the power of divination possessed by cooks, but also to the fact that these latter, when they go every evening to the train for a supply of eatables, are brought in contact with the drivers who have come from the rear.

Milliard, the postman of the company, arrives with two bags full of letters. Everybody rushes up to him. These are the first letters that have reached us since we left Humes. Milliard calls out the names. All round him are the chief corporals of the squadron who answer "Present!" for the men, and often, alas! "Dead!" "Wounded!" or "Missing!"

Regarding the letters, a brilliant idea has at last entered Roberty's brain. He says: "If each company's letters are called out before the men of the company, instead of shouting them before an indiscriminate mass or before nobody at all, the letters themselves and those for whom they are destined would have a better chance of being brought together." The commander has sanctioned a trial of the system. Sergeant Milliard, of the 24th, searches in the bags. Knowing us well by name, he finds our letters. Wonderful! Some of the men burst into tears; others slip away, their trembling hands grasping the precious missives on which the familiar handwriting is seen.

Such excess of happiness emboldens one, and Milliard is asked, though in somewhat hesitating accents—

"Suppose I entrust you with a letter, what will become of it?"

"I will take it to the postman's van for you."

The deuce!

"And you think it will reach its destination?"

"Certainly; I can promise you that."

Thereupon the letter is timidly placed in Milliard's hands.

About five in the afternoon, Charensac assures us with a knowing air—

"Castelnau has put off the attack."

Friday, 25th; Saturday, 26th; Sunday, 27th September.

We recross the Aisne and again begin to dig holes. The trenches are soon deep enough, covered with foliage. We rest, surrounded by picks and shovels. It is very hot. Some write or talk; others roll about on the grass.

The shells mostly pass far above our heads. Of a sudden, however, three of them burst too near to be pleasant. Quickly returning to our holes, we form a carapace. Is it over? No, a fourth explosion is heard. But no harm is done.

Monday, 28th September.

The night is spent guarding the bridge of boats so heroically defended on the 20th by a company of engineers. No incident worth mentioning; a few spent bullets fall near the sentry-box.

In the morning we mount to the trenches and the day is spent idling about the grass. We have surrounded a corner of the meadow with branches of trees, sharpened and driven into the ground. No enemy, however excellent his observation glasses, could possibly discover our whereabouts. It is almost as peaceful as under the apple-tree of *Père Achille*. A fencing match, with sticks for swords.

Whenever the hum of an aeroplane is heard, the usual cry is raised—

"An aeroplane! Quick! To earth!"

Like rabbits we run and hide in our holes.

Jules appears, carrying a hen which he has come across somewhere and which

Varlet has cooked without drawing or eviscerating it. The mistake is regrettable. All the same, Corporal Belin goes too far in refusing his share, protesting he will not eat a morsel of "that filth." Varlet gets vexed. Being accustomed to speak at public meetings, he has a tongue. But Belin, who has served nine years in the Foreign Legion, has principles of his own.

"I have served in Morocco and Western Algeria," he says, "and have often gone without food altogether, but I have never seen any one cook a hen undrawn."

And he sticks to his opinion.

Thereupon Varlet calls him a savage.

"A savage!" shrieks Belin, "a savage because I refuse to eat a hen's entrails!"

The dispute becomes embittered. Varlet forgets his position. Belin points to his red stripes and furiously sputters out threats.

The lieutenant intervenes and peace is made. Varlet acknowledges that it would have been better to draw the fowl, whilst Belin consents to eat a wing without making a wry face about it.

Tuesday, 29th; Wednesday, 30th September.

For the time being, at all events, the sector is to be organized for the defensive. The positions held by the enemy before Fontenoy can only be taken, we are informed, by siege. The Germans have constructed very strong trenches and lodged their reserves in grottoes sheltered from all possible bombardment, i.e. in subterranean quarries of which there are several in these parts.

On the other hand, the Russians are neither in Berlin nor anywhere near it.... *Allons!* The war will not come to an end next month.

Evidently in Paris they are considering the possibility of a winter campaign. Ladies are knitting woollen vests for us!

We shall see. In a soldier's life one must not dwell too much on the future, seeing that the entire situation may change from day to day.

Thursday, 1st October.

At dawn we leave for Le Châtelet, a hamlet perched on the heights overlooking the left bank of the Aisne, in front of Vic. A magnificent view over the valley. The company is to remain quartered here several weeks, to organize the position. The farm in which we are to lodge is surrounded by beautiful meadows.

We sleep on mattresses in a loft. If our stay here is to be prolonged, I feel that I shall resume my old habits of cleanliness.

Friday, 2nd October.

Alas! Réveillé at two in the morning. The situation has changed. The 24th goes down to Gorgny, and with arms piled and haversacks on the ground, is waiting in the enclosure of the château. At five comes the order to depart. *En route* for Courmelles, somewhere to the south of Soissons.

A forced march of thirty kilometres through the night. At eleven o'clock we reach Courmelles, utterly worn out. Whilst waiting until our quarters are ready, we lie down *pêle-mêle* on the road alongside the houses. A Moroccan brigade crosses the village. The moonlight projects a bluish light on to the rapid and silent march of these men, wrapped in great hoods and with enormous haversacks towering above their heads: Mâtho's mercenaries. They are going in a northerly direction.

The squadron sleeps in a loft abounding in straw. To cover my body I have a potato sack, which I use as a hood in the daytime.

Saturday, 3rd October.

At ten in the morning we are still asleep, snugly ensconced in the straw. For a month we have not once had a sufficiency of sleep.

Lieutenant Roberty summons us: Reymond, Maxence, Verrier and myself. His room is at our disposal for a wash and a change of linen. For this evening he converts his bed into two and shares it with us.

I receive a wire from Paris, which was dispatched on the 18th of September. A fortnight on the way! Evidently letters take less time: a good thing, too!

Many of the houses in Courmelles have been abandoned. In one of them the squadron makes arrangements for meals, a corporal—in ordinary life a mountebank—acting as cook. He whistles a number of popular airs whilst making a fricassee of three rabbits in an iron foot-pan. It is dinner-time. The rabbits are not fit to eat; they are burnt, and have an after-taste of soap. We turn up our noses, and I am the only one willing to taste the stew. I become nicknamed "the eater of filthy food," but this does not trouble me in the slightest. Luckily there is an enormous dish of fried potatoes, and the baker has consented to sell us some hot white bread.

Varlet and Charensac have gone for a stroll to Soissons. They had to cut across fields to escape the gendarmes, who pursued them a considerable distance. They return hot and perspiring, greatly excited, and laden with rare dainties: any quantity of tobacco, chocolate, preserves, dubbing, writing-paper, couch grass brushes and pipes.

Soissons is filled with English soldiers and business seems very thriving. The town is exceedingly animated. Every one is overjoyed at the thought that the place is free of the enemy.

Sunday, 4th October.

Still resting. Optimists assure us that the regiment is to stay a month at Courmelles.

Letters long overdue now arrive along with the first parcels. One of them contains butter!

Roberty's orderly, Jules, is nothing if not bold. Under the pretext that it is Sunday, he offers to shave us and cut our hair. He has not the faintest idea of the hair-dresser's art, though he is delighted at his prospective occupation. I am his first victim. The villain manages to convert my hair into a miniature staircase.

Then he shaves me, and to the accompaniment of such remarks as "That's right!" "I'm improving!" he tears away the skin along with the hair. Terrified, I have not even the courage to request him to stop. The operation ended, I press little pads of wadding on to my bleeding chin and make my escape. My comrades hold their sides with laughter, Jules chuckles with pride and vanity as he asks—

"Next one?"

The lieutenant sends for me—

"Guess who's here?"

"A civilian?"

"Come down and see."

Girard! Maxime Girard of the *Figaro*. I press his hands with mingled affection and violence. After repeating a dozen times: "How small the world is, after all! To think of seeing you here!" we plunge at once into intimate conversation.

Girard is even dirtier than I am. His face is entirely covered with a thick layer of dust. Nose and trousers are of the same greyish tint. Cheeks and chin are covered with a downy beard. His coat possesses only one row of buttons, but he is just as much a gentleman as ever he was.

The mountebank corporal has promised to provide a good dinner; we may therefore invite Girard. He visits the kitchen. On seeing that we have at our disposal glasses and plates, dishes and a soup-tureen, a table and chairs, he slips away and only returns at the dinner-hour, shaven, brushed and washed, a man of the world.

After coffee, benedictine, cigars and pipes. Girard relates his campaigns, which resemble our own: bullets and shells, marches, orders and counter-orders, dust and mud; wounded men passing to the rear and comrades falling dead. Then the precipitate falling back of the Germans, the welcome halting-places where you shake off all your troubles and worries so successfully that you actually think the war is over!

Monday, 5th October.

On to the plain from which one gains a sight of Soissons, the battalion mounts to visit some old German trenches. There is a fine view of the town and of the cathedral of Saint-Jean-des-Vignes, one tower of which has been shot away. Firing continues away towards the north.

Three English companies are drilling: array in skirmish line, advance against hostile fire, muster in two rows. The various movements are carried through with all the regularity and precision of a ballet dance.

The thirteenth-century church at Courmelles is delightful to behold; the apse being pure Roman. We visit it as tourists.

CHAPTER VII

OUR FIRST TRENCHES

Tuesday, 6th October.

The commander of the company announces that the regiment is to take the first line, to relieve the English in the trenches of Bucy-le-Long. We set off gaily at seven in the evening, after taking an affectionate leave of Girard.

Out in the open, the order comes to fling away our cigarettes. Things are becoming serious. We pass through the suburbs of Soissons; the cathedral appears dimly in the moonlight. At the corner of a street lies a dead horse. All along the main road are the bivouacs of Alpine troops. Vénizel. Here the English are guarding a level-crossing; strapping fellows in khaki, who smoke pipes and shout "Good-night!" to us. Then a bridge, the crossing of the Aisne, an open plain, a village, a steep hill, a wood as dark as Hades. In spite of the cold wind we are perspiring freely. It is nearly midnight. We reach a sort of semi-circle dotted with sheds or huts made of the branches of trees. The Germans, it appears, are six hundred yards distant. Not a shot is fired. The night is very clear.

The company halts, and the men immediately lie down flat, with rifles ready, awaiting orders.

Roberty calls for two volunteers from each squadron to go on post duty. Reymond and I stand up, and Belin goes with us. The English officer, who appoints us our places, looks very elegant in his cloak, which falls behind in broad folds; he leans on a large stick, walks briskly, and gives his orders and directions with the utmost courtesy and consideration.

Several hundred yards forward, in the direction of the enemy. Here is the post line; every two hundred yards a group of six English soldiers is lying flat on the ground amongst the beetroots, alongside of the road. They stand erect and we take their places. We admire these fine-looking soldiers, so well-equipped and under perfect discipline. In a low tone of voice the officer gives the order to fire upon everything that passes before us.

Yesterday the English captured a German patrol.

To take post duty at night, in an unfamiliar sector, is a novel experience. For the first time you have the impression that you are waging war: war such as your imagination depicted it, war according to the story-books of your boyhood.

Corporal Belin explains that we must be careful not to take the waving of a beetroot leaf for the advance of an enemy.

Every two minutes he counts off: one! and each man must answer in file: two, three, four, five, six.

Thus he makes sure that no one is asleep. The prolonged whistle of the bullets as they pass makes us open our eyes. We can hear dull sounds in front of us: the Germans are camping, cutting down trees. A dog barks. Carts rumble along: the German supplies, no doubt. The roar of cannon in the distance.

It is bitterly cold. Hoar-frost shows itself on our coats and on the beetroots. My jacket is in my haversack: I take it out and tie it round my neck by the sleeves. Impossible to keep warm.

Reymond passes me a small bottle.

"Taste. This must be something especially good; it comes from home."

I take a good drink.

"Gracious! How strong it is! And what a strange taste!"

It is Reymond's turn to drink, he smacks his lips and reflects. Finally he says—

"I believe it's arnica."

We do our best to keep awake. Belin counts: One! I answer: Two, and a snore escapes me. A dig in the ribs brings me back to the reality of things.

"Well! Didn't I say: 'Two'?"

"You did," whispers Belin ironically; "but you said it with a snore."

"Even if I snore, I don't fall asleep."

"That's news to me," affirms Belin with all the authority of his nine years' campaigns.

The better to keep awake, we begin to talk. Reymond asks a question.

"I say, Belin, this is a real outpost, is it not?"

"Certainly."

"In case of attack, what becomes of the outposts?"

"In case of attack, the outposts are invariably sacrificed," answers Belin with calm assurance.

Wednesday, 7th October.

At five o'clock Belin takes us back to the rear. We are dreadfully cold and our teeth are chattering. A good drink of hot coffee, followed by a mouthful of brandy, and we fall asleep.

The position dominating Bucy-le-Long and the plain of Vénizel was carried last month by the English and a body of Zouaves. They drove the Germans from the valley back to the heights and only halted on reaching a plain which extends to the horizon, a vast field of beetroots cut by the main road between Maubeuge and Paris.

The English trenches lay between the hill and the wood. Here and there are large shelters for seven or eight men, a sort of rabbit-hutch; the roofs, made of the trunk's of trees, are covered with a thick layer of earth.

In front of the road, pickets planted in the field in quincunx form and connected together by wire.

Here and there on the wires hang empty preserve tins, which strike against each other at the slightest movement. If a hostile patrol reaches the wire-work, it starts the warning tins, and the alarm is given. This system of defence we look upon as both formidable and ingenious.

Everywhere we find evidences of English comfort: the road leading to the verge of the wood is swept and kept in perfect order; the descending footpaths are improved with wooden stairs and balustrades, signposts indicate the direction of the village, of lavatories, etc. On the slope of the hill are numerous sheds made of boughs, for the men of the reserve company. Half-way up is a wash-house, surrounded by flat stones and shaded by oaks. The English have brought spring water, emptying it into large wooden buckets, so that it is possible to have a bath whenever one pleases.

We explore this negro "exhibition" sort of village. The enemy is a few hundred yards distant, though nothing makes us anticipate an attack. A dead calm, magnificent weather, a soft light gilding the oaks, beeches and the birch-trees now reddening with the autumn tints.

Our allies and predecessors have left behind quantities of provisions, tins of corned beef, gallons of whisky and cigarettes. The discovery of such wealth fills us with childish joy. Decidedly the first line is an abode of delight, a peaceful haven of rest.

The shelters assigned to Roberty's section are large and substantial, if not very airy. You enter on all-fours through an opening less than thirty inches square. This opening serves both as door and window; it is closed by a screen made of leafy twigs.

"I believe we've struck the vein," says some one, signifying that we have found a veritable mine of prosperity and happiness.

Guard duty is not very tiring: a couple of hours by day, and the same number by night.

Thursday, 8th October.

The very last thing we expected was a holiday. Nothing to do but sleep and dream, rise late, prattle to one another and write letters. We lounge about, chatting with the cooks who have lit their fires in some secluded glade; or else, lying smoking on the grass, gaze upon the smiling village. In the background, at the other end of the valley, hills ascending into the grey-blue of the sky. The landscape somewhat commonplace; though charming, there is nothing theatrical about it.

It is so mild that I take a tub in the open air. To crown our happiness, the postman brings us a number of letters and parcels.

The German shells pass high above our heads and come crashing down all over Bucy.

Even night sentry duty is a pleasure, consisting as it does of a stroll along the road, with some one to talk to all the while. This is the only time in the day when one can chat at one's ease, talk of Paris and one's family, exchange ideas which have no bearing on the next meal or the state of one's stomach. Our safety is assured by the outposts. A glorious moonlight night, the peace of which is but emphasized by the firing of the sentries.

Friday, 9th October.

We have not yet received our coverings; the consequence being that we awake with frozen limbs. This morning, the country is white with hoar-frost. Belin makes us chocolate in the morning, a rice pudding at noon, and tea at four. Considerable freedom is allowed in the composition of the meals, which last three hours. At lunch we begin with sardines and eggs, followed by apple marmalade. Then Jules arrives from Bucy, bringing with him a roasted fowl, every morsel of which we eat. Lastly, the cooks of the squadron bring soup and coffee.

War is full of unexpected incidents: a month of the second line had utterly exhausted us; whereas the close proximity of the enemy now gives us the impression of a picnic.... All the same, one of the outpost men has just been killed.

At ten in the evening, the 352nd is relieved and leaves the first line for a three days' rest in the rear. We are broken-hearted at the prospect.

The battalion is quartered at Acy-le-Haut, on the left bank of the Aisne.

Saturday, 10th; Sunday, 11th; and Monday, 12th October.

Jules has found for Roberty, Maxence, Reymond, Verrier and myself, a house where the mistress consents to cook for us and lend us mattresses. Varlet, who is to remain at the official quarters in his capacity as cook, promises to warn us in case of alarm. Our landlady looks after us like a mother; for lunch she serves us with roast veal, and for dinner with beef stewed in *daube*. These we shall look back upon amongst our souvenirs of the war....

On Sunday morning, Gabriel, a sergeant of the 21st, former quartermaster of the 27th at Humes, was killed at drill! Whilst rectifying the position of one of his men, he shook the rifle which was still loaded. The shot went off without the trigger, which was very loose, being touched. The poor fellow received the bullet full in the mouth.

The interment takes place in the afternoon. The coffin is carried through the streets of Acy. All the women of the village have brought flowers. Behind the body walks Belin, holding up the cross, his Moroccan and Algerian medals on his breast. Gabriel was head of the section: his men follow with hastily prepared wreaths. The 21st company renders the usual funeral honours.

Absolution is pronounced in the church. The windows are broken to pieces; their debris still hang from the bays.

The silence is profound. Gabriel was much loved and willingly obeyed. This very week he was to have been appointed sub-lieutenant. Nothing is more heart-breaking than to die by accident in war.

On Monday evening we return to the trenches. There is a rumour that the Germans have taken Antwerp.

Tuesday, 13th October.

When it rains, the first line loses its charm. The whole day must be spent lying flat on the ground, for the ceiling of the dug-out is too low to allow of a sitting posture. In wet weather the hours spent on sentry duty pass very slowly.

This evening, at seven, whilst quietly chattering away by lantern-light, firing is heard on the left. We look at one another. The firing draws nearer.

Roberty orders us to pick up our rifles. We are soon running along the road, slightly crouching forward, for the bullets strike branches of trees on a level with our heads.

We rejoin the rest of the section and take aim. Belin hesitates before ordering us to fire.

"Wait until we see the lights of the enemy's fire."

But no light appears, and after half an hour the firing inexplicably ceases. We return. At midnight another alarm, as incomprehensible as the former. Three or four men are wounded. The utmost calm throughout the rest of the night.

Wednesday, 14th; Thursday, 15th; Friday, 16th; Saturday, 17th October.

We are evidently carrying on a siege war, though of course no one expected that it would be a ride over. Apart from the four hours' sentry duty, we have nothing to do. Jules continues to go backwards and forwards between the trenches and Bucy for supplies. The fire for our own private cooking is not allowed to die out.

Last night Reymond and myself were up from one till three. A terrible artillery duel was being fought in the right sector, towards Vailly. The sky was streaked with great flashes of light. No firing on our side.

We are sitting close to our dug-out, discussing Wagner, rifle in hand. The conversation, which began on a low key, quickly grows animated, and the hum of our voices goes out upon the night air. Suddenly the leafy screen, which serves as a door, divides, and Roberty appears on all-fours. His head is enveloped in a *passe-montagne* and the little we see of his face expresses annoyance and irritation.

"Aren't you two going to hold your tongues?"

"Well, we are only having a word or two. Cannot one talk in war-time?"

"You've been preventing me from sleeping the last quarter of an hour, with your intellectual...."

"Intellectual, indeed! Didn't you go to the *Ecole Normale* as a boy?"

"You're a couple of idiots. If I hear another word, you must take the consequences."

He disappears into his kennel. We resume our conversation, though almost in a whisper.

Sunday, 18th October.

The regiment quarters on the other bank of the Aisne, at Billy. Jules has gone on in advance with some of the men, to make preparations. He finds a suitable house. We take advantage of the darkness to slip away without a sound, after telling the rest of the squadron where to find us in case of alarm. The house is comfortable, and there are beds in it. Roberty, feeling unwell, rests on one of them.

Monday, 19th October.

What an extraordinary war! We have had nothing to do for three weeks!

To-day: more "labour" to ensure bodily cleanliness.

At night we loiter slipshod about the house and try to read. We are bored to death.

Tuesday, 20th; Wednesday, 21st; Thursday, 22nd; Friday, 23rd October.

The same monotonous idle life in quarters. A couple of hours' exercise in the morning. Review in the afternoon: hair review, for instance. Before the men, bare-headed and standing at attention, passes the lieutenant, who judges whether or not each individual's hair is of the regulation length. With certain dishevelled shocks facing him, he makes a gesture indicative of despair, as though he would conjure them away. The barber follows, note-book in hand, jotting down the names of those who are to pass through his hands.

What is the reason of this aversion for the clipper? And why does the soldier insist on being long-haired? Is it because the ancient Gauls were long-haired? Anyhow, there is an eternal struggle between the officers, solicitous of the men's health, and the *poilus*, who think more of the esthetic side of the matter—generally a debatable one.

There is again a rumour that our regiment is to be sent for a rest into the centre of France. The cooks of the first squadron mention Bourges; those of the ninth, Tours.

Another rumour is that Germany is proposing peace to Russia.

Saturday, 24th October.

As we see from letters and newspapers, civilians share in all the agitation and excitement of the war. We are out of all this. By the aid of successive communiqués, those left behind follow the various incidents of the great war on all the fronts at once. Perhaps, too, they receive the *Bulletin des Armées*, not a single number of which we have yet seen....

They will not have lost a crumb of information! Whereas for a month and a half we have been moving from quarters to outposts and back again, thinking of nothing but eating and drinking, sleeping and resisting cold. At bottom, nothing more resembles the army on a peace footing than the army on a war footing: fatigue duty, reviews, cleaning and polishing arms, sentry duty, and musters. Nor can the soldier be said to be more serious.... To-morrow, it may be, we shall have to leave the trenches and fight. Good, that is our business, the thing we are here to do. When the moment comes, shall we feel ourselves carried away in a whirl of excitement, as civilians do? Nothing of the kind. We shall crawl along the ground, make a few rushes, perhaps have a fall, though without seeing or understanding anything. And on the morrow, unless we are dead, we shall return to oblivion.

Even courage—and there *is* such a thing—is but a matter of habit, one might almost say of negligence. We do not excite ourselves about shells; if we did, life would be altogether impossible; the French soldier will not admit that anything should make a complete change in his existence. Accordingly, he comes and goes, gets into and out of scrapes and difficulties as though nothing mattered.

But we *do* get bored, because present-day warfare is colourless and dull, like our uniforms. Those at home, however, suppose us to be in the thick of it all the time, standing with bayonet fixed and head flung back, ferocious and hirsute, blood-stained and sublime. Is it in this light that history will depict us? I hope not, both for its own sake and for our own.

Now I must be off to clean some potatoes. The battalion is returning to the trenches shortly.

CHAPTER VIII

TWENTY-TWO DAYS IN THE TRENCHES

Sunday, 25th October.

Roberty, our lieutenant, has been evacuated. We saw him leave in the ambulance. We are very sorry, as he is the first friend to drop out of our life so far.

Two months' intimacy, pleasure and pain shared hourly by us all, have enabled us to appreciate at his true worth this officer with whom Reymond and myself have been on the most intimate terms, and who valued his rank only in so far as it enabled him to make the life of his men more tolerable. I am not speaking merely of ourselves, his close friends; every soldier of the section did more than obey him. They dreaded his displeasure, and looked quite discomfited if by any chance they had made him angry. Roberty slept on straw with the first squadron, partaking of the same food as the rest. He cheerfully performed every duty that fell to an officer's lot.

Every evening, in the trenches, he went himself to arrange about the outposts. His task finished, he would come back to us in our shelter and engage in a friendly chat and smoke.

"Even in the Foreign Legion," remarked Belin, "I never saw that done."

Raising his index finger, he added—

"But though he made himself one of us, I never respected any officer more than I respected him."

No, we were not very gay last night as we gathered sorrowfully round our lieutenant's bed.

"So it's decided that you are to go?" I said to him. "Well, there'll be precious little fun in fighting with you away!"

He was suffering much, and made no answer. When, however, the stretcher-bearers came for him, he spoke to us somewhat after the fashion in which Mazarin, on his death-bed, recommended Colbert to the youthful Louis XIV—

"My children, though I have done much for you, I crown all my kindness by leaving you Jules. You have seen him at work; he has every possible vice. Make use of his virtues as well."

Once more we admired the goodness and generosity of our kind chief, whom, alas! we were to lose. Our last words were—

"Thanks for everything. You have been a real brother to us, and we will never forget you."

Then the ambulance carried him off. Immediately afterwards we found Jules in a corner, looking the picture of despair. The lieutenant's departure was for him the end of a dream.

"Come here, Jules. The lieutenant has advised us to take you along. Will you come?"

"Of course," replied Jules. "We shall get along all right. Just now the adjutant asked me if I would do something for him. He did not even look at me! And that, after being the lieutenant's orderly! Naturally I would rather be with you."

With Roberty away, one of the charms of the war has disappeared. Everybody in the section looks troubled and careworn. Never again shall we see his like!

Our friend Varlet takes off his apron as a sign of mourning. He has been the cook of the squadron.

"The lieutenant," he says, "is the first man I ever took pleasure in obeying. Now that he is gone, I will cook no more!"

Monday, 26th October.

It may be on account of the departure of the lieutenant, anyhow, the jovial pleasant life of the past no longer obtains in the first line.

This morning we are told to dig a branch, i.e. a winding passage between five and six feet in height, which will link up the old English trenches with the outpost line. The enemy is firing.

A sergeant, who left Humes with the Roberty detachment, receives a bullet in his head. The stretcher-bearers who carry him off pass right in front of us. The wounded man looks as lifeless as a log. The dressing about his forehead is red with blood. We salute, and then dig away with pick and shovel harder than ever.

At nightfall the company occupies a new sector in a wood, on the top of a hill-ock. Here there are no more trenches, but instead, along the road which ascends and descends between the trees, are huts made of branches and earth, capable of sheltering three of us at most.

Tuesday, 27th October.

A day of rest, with the sun shining upon us. We have received blankets and coverings. They are very welcome.

Artillery duel. The game has its rules. This morning, for instance, it is the Germans who silence the French artillery; i.e. they cover with projectiles our supposed emplacements or sites. Whilst this is happening, our gunners leave their cannons deep buried in the ground and go away for a quiet pipe in a safe shelter. When the Germans cease firing the French will begin. Then the maddening crack of the 75's, the hoarse coughing sound of the 105's, and the 155's will indicate that the turn of the French artillery has come to reduce the enemy to silence.

All this firing goes on far above the head of the foot-soldier. Still, it is to be hoped that no shot, fired too short, may fall on our group and involve us in the discussion, in spite of ourselves.

Whilst this cannonade is going on we write letters, looking up from time to time to see where the little puffs of smoke mark the explosions.

Wednesday, 28th October.

A bad night. Yesterday, at muster, Sergeant Chaboy explains—

"The first and second squadrons are ordered to leave the trenches. You will advance 150 yards nearer the enemy. There you will dig an advance trench. You will have your work cut out to be completely underground by dawn. You understand?"

It is quite clear. At nine o'clock the half-section is mustered. It has rained, and the road through the wood is muddy and slippery. A few resounding falls. We reach the entrance of the winding passage. Some parts are so narrow that we cannot negotiate them either front face or sideways, because of haversack and *musette*. Thereupon we force our way through, causing clods of earth to fall to the bottom. The depth of the branch is not the same throughout; from time to time we have to proceed on all-fours. A *gamelle*, a bayonet or a can are noisy objects which respond to the slightest touch.

On reaching the outpost trenches the men scale the parapet. This must be done quickly and in silence. At the faintest sound the Germans would begin a hellish fire; the French would return it, and between the two we should be swept away.

The sergeant says in low tones—

"This is the spot. Crouch down and begin."

Some of the men have shovels, others work with knives and bayonets, but principally with their hands. In half an hour every man has erected a small parapet.

Perspiration is pouring from us. At that moment it begins to rain. We continue to dig.

In front of the workers some of the men keep watch, hidden in the beetroots. They try to see through the darkness if anything stirs in front.

About two in the morning my hole is about three feet deep, and is protected by nearly two feet of earth. I am covered with mud. Utterly exhausted, I fling myself down by the side of the trench, and, wrapping my cover over my head to protect me from the rain, I fall into a heavy sleep and begin to snore. My neighbour wakes me with a crack on the head from his shovel handle.

"Idiot! do you want them to use us as a target?" he remarks affably.

"I'm too sleepy to care whether they do or not."

Whereupon I turn over on to my side and fall asleep again. An hour afterwards I awake, quite frozen, and begin to dig with renewed vigour. The deeper the trench becomes the fewer precautions do we take. At dawn we chatter and laugh aloud. The Germans make no sign of life; perhaps they are afraid of the rain.

What luck! We are relieved by two fresh squadrons. We reach the second line, listening as we go to the good-humoured banter of men who have spent the night under cover.

A pretty picture we make! For a hood I have flung over my head a potato-sack, and over my shoulders a wet bed-cover, as our grandmothers used to do with their cashmere shawls. Hands and coats, *képis* and puttees are all covered with sticky yellow mud, whilst our rifles are useless, owing to the barrel being stopped up and the mechanism filled with earth.

Thursday, 29th October.

The 24th have spent the night in the grotto, the paradise of the trench. The grotto is the name we have given to a deep subterranean quarry, whose passages, thirty feet in height, penetrate right into the hillock.

It has three passages. In the right one a room appears as though it had been specially constructed for our squadron; this we win by main force. Of course, it is as dark as an oven, so we fix wax candles in the jutting ledges. A bayonet dug into the ground with a candle tied on to the handle is used by such as want a light for their own personal use.

Here we are in perfect safety. This is one of the few places on the front where one is completely sheltered from any kind of projectile. In these depths we scarcely hear the roar of the cannon at all.

At nightfall the entrance assumes quite a romantic aspect: a Hindu temple or Egyptian hypogeum, with its blue shadows and vivid lights. By moonlight it would make a fitting scene for the witches in Macbeth. Not long ago we should have spoken of Fafner's cave, *Fafner's Höhle*!

In the interior the sharp-edged stone also gives the impression of theatrical cardboard scenery; the atmosphere is that of the Quarter: shouts, songs, and laughter, ringing commands echoed by the sonorous vaults—

"The 24th, get the potatoes ready!"

"Muster for fatigue duty!"

And so on. No need to speak in whispers or to put oneself under the slightest restraint. This is a real place of refuge, rendered neutral by nature, and in the direct line of fire. Neither rain nor shot has any chance at all.

Until further orders the company will spend one night in the trenches and one in the grotto alternately.

The letters! Milliard the postman's service has become an official one. Henriot has been appointed to help him. No fear of this latter botching the correspondence; he passes the whole of his time in writing endless letters which his wife answers with equal patience and enthusiasm. Whenever by chance the post brings him nothing, Henriot falls into a state of grim silence and replies to all questions with an injured sneer.

Friday, 30th October.

Since last evening there has been a continuous fusillade in the direction of the fort of Condé. The Germans are furiously bombarding the second line of our sector. A convoy of munitions passes along the road. Two gunners are wounded. We hear them cry out in the night—

"This way, comrades! Help! Ah! ah!"

An aeroplane skims over the lines. We judge by the sound of the motor that it is flying very low.

At daybreak the bombardment redoubles in intensity, and continues all day long. Our batteries reply, the 155's, as they pass over the trenches, making a sound which resembles the rustling of a gigantic silk dress.

Silence follows. We needed it badly. Fortunately, the company sleeps in the grotto. At eight o'clock, well wrapped in their bed-covers and with a muffler round the neck and head resting on haversack, the men sleep the sleep of perfect security.

Saturday, 31st October.

The section is on picket. Every time an aeroplane passes and the lieutenant, armed with his glasses, declares it to belong to the enemy, we fire at it. From time to time the machine may pitch a little, or ascend out of reach. Assuredly, this is not the sort of game for foot-soldiers.

The commander of the company to-day addressed us as follows—

"Above the grotto are buried four Englishmen, killed here last month. On All Saints' Day you would not like their tombs, which you have seen so often, to appear neglected. Make some wreaths, and we will all go together and place them on the graves of those who died in defence of our soil. It is not your commander, it is your comrade who asks this of you."

The men silently leave the ranks and set out into the wood. In less than an hour they have made up beautiful wreaths of ivy and holly. Chrysanthemums have been found in a garden which the Germans had forgotten to plunder. The graves, indicated by a couple of crosses, have become pretty tombs, similar to those one sees in a village cemetery.

The entire company lined up on the hillock for the simple ceremony. Our lieutenant saluted in memory of our unknown brothers who have given their lives for France. We shouted aloud: *"Vive l'Angleterre!"* The picket rendered the honours due, and each man returned to his post.

These dead heroes are Lieutenant B. MacCuire and Privates H.C. Dover, R. Byrne, and Ford, of the Royal Dublin Fusiliers.

In offering these flowers to their memory, our thoughts were directed to the mourning families of the dead soldiers.

Sunday, 1st November.

A hot sun and a brilliant day, the right weather for a fête. The first line is calmer than ever. Not a cannon shot is heard.

Monday, 2nd November.

Three months since mobilization took place. We must allow for another three months before peace is declared. I have a row with Reymond because he pushed me and upset my coffee. Quarrel. Reymond is chosen to go on outpost duty; I ask permission to accompany him. Reconciliation. Corporal Davor conducts us through the winding passages, comes out in the field of beetroot, gets lost and makes straight for the German lines. He discovers his mistake just in time and we beat a retreat. Sergeant Chaboy, making his round, stops to have a few words with us.

"Expect to be fired upon shortly," he says. "An attack is brewing from the direction of Condé."

After a silence, he adds—

"If the shells fall in too great numbers you may withdraw."

"When do shells fall in too great numbers for an outpost?" asks the corporal timidly.

With a vague gesture, the sergeant leaves us to solve the problem ourselves.

The moon is at the full, and it is so light that Reymond is able to make a sketch and I to write a letter, as we await the promised attack. Nothing happens, however. Sleep is our only enemy. Reymond puts on his poncho, wraps a red silk handkerchief round his head, and, pretending to strum away on a shovel as though it were a mandolin, softly hums a *malagueña*.

Tuesday, 3rd November.

The lieutenant calls out—

"I want some one with his wits about him to act as telephonist at the artillery observation post."

I modestly step forward.

After a moment's hesitation the lieutenant remarks—

"Good! Off you go."

I reach the first line trench. An emplacement two yards square has been dug in the trench branch and covered with corrugated sheet-iron. An artillery captain is seated here on a high stool looking through a telescope. By his side is the telephone.

The captain explains—

"I am off to inspect my battery. During my absence, sit here and keep your eyes glued to the telescope. What you see is one of the entrances of the fort of Condé, about five kilometres distant. If you find the enemy mustering, telephone immediately. The spot is marked, our guns will be fired, and you will be able to see what happens."

I take up my post. After a short time small silhouettes begin to move about within the field of vision. Gradually I make out German foot-soldiers coming and going unarmed. Evidently they have mustered for some fatigue duty or other. For the first time there appears before my eyes the horrifying spectacle of invasion—the enemy's forces moving about on French territory as though it were their own.

Quitting the telescope, I spring to the telephone.

"Battery number 90!... *Mon capitaine*, a muster is forming.... Yes, at the very spot you mentioned."

Four almost simultaneous detonations from the battery. Whilst the salvo is on its way I return to the telescope; the four shells fall right on the muster, raising into the air enormous columns of earth. The smoke dissipates. Staring with all my eyes, I see little grey figures scatter in every direction. Five cavalry, riding just outside the zone of explosion, dig their spurs into their horses' sides and flee. Not a living soul to be seen. Looking hard, I imagine I notice dead bodies on the ground.

Apparently, at the spot under surveillance, there are works to be completed, for on three occasions that morning fresh musters form. I do not succeed in making out what they are doing, but on each occasion a salvo from the battery scatters them.

The captain to whom I wire the results is delighted.

"Don't let them go," he answers. "Any movement in the spot marked will be dealt with as the others have been. They have no idea where we are."

I return to my watch. A mere foot-soldier in charge of a battery may well feel proud. How nice to be some one "with his wits about him."

Wednesday, 4th; Thursday, 5th November.

My rôle as observer is rendered ineffectual by a dense mist.

Alpine infantry from the *Midi* relieve us. The company goes down to quarter at Bucy-le-Long. We have now been in the trenches twelve days. None the less do we receive the order to "be ready for every eventuality."

Friday, 6th November.

After a passable night in the cellar of a house in ruins, we send out Jules, as usual, to find decent lodging for us. He does so and brings us to see it. It is a large bedroom where it is possible for us to remove our boots, change our linen, shave, and generally make ourselves presentable. The luncheon is a substantial one. Seated round the table, we look almost like normal human beings once more. Besides, our hands are actually clean!

This night, our undressed carcasses slip into white bed-clothes. It is two months since we have had such a treat!

Saturday, 7th November.

At six in the morning Varlet enters like a whirlwind—

"Get up at once, lazy-bones! Muster in half an hour."

"Bah! You're joking!"

"Come now; quick, into your clothes! We are going back to the trenches."

So this is the promised eventuality!

At half-past six the company musters in a farmyard. The order to leave has not yet come. Seated on our haversacks, we snatch a hasty breakfast. Fortunately, Reymond has received some good cigars, which he passes round. He sings us a Spanish song—

> *Padre capucino mata su mujer*
> *La corta en pedazos, la pone a cocer*
> *Gente que pasaba olia tocino:*
> *Era la mujer del padre capucino.*

This means: "The Capuchin monk has killed his wife, cut her in pieces and set her to cook. The passers-by say there is a smell of burning fat. That's what is left of the wife of the Capuchin monk."

This absurd song puts us in good humour.

At three o'clock, *en route* for the trenches. The men say to one another—

"We are off at last."

For the moment at least the company is to support the batteries installed in the wood above the road from Bucy to Margival. The 75's are booming away. What is going to happen? Nothing at all. Night falls. We sit or lie on the ground along the road awaiting orders, chatting, smoking, and jesting to kill time. Milliard and Henriot mount the hill. We prepare to receive them. But how is it that they are armed and equipped? Above all, why do they come empty-handed? And that, just at the time we expect our letters? Milliard simply remarks—

"Well, we're here."

Henriot is in one of his silent moods; we can get nothing out of him.

"Where are the letters?"

"Letters, letters," says Milliard, irritated, "you all think of nothing but your letters."

This reply fills us with consternation. Something serious must have happened for our postman to speak in this strain.

Some one remarks peevishly—

"The company is to attack this evening or to-morrow morning. If any one gets a bullet through the head and dies without receiving his letters it will be all your fault."

Milliard makes a gesture expressive of regret.

"You see," he confesses timidly, "Henriot and I have just heard that the 24th is to attack, and so we simply left the letters to look after themselves. We thought you might not be pleased; but then, really, we had not the heart to remain behind."

Henriot the taciturn screws up his courage to add a final sentence—

"We could not leave our mates to be killed all by themselves."

Then a harsh voice is heard saying—

"It's all very fine to come along and get killed with one's comrades. But if you fall, there will be no one to attend to the correspondence. And once more our letters will be left lying about anywhere! You've thought only of yourselves in the whole matter."

At seven o'clock the 24th retires to the grotto to sleep.

Sunday, 8th November.

Sabbath rest until five in the evening. Evidently there is to be an attack. Instead of returning to our huts in the wood, we follow the path leading to Crouy alongside of our former trenches. At half-past six firing is heard; our infantry are beginning the assault. Violent cannonade on both sides. Lights flash through the dark sky. Lying on our backs, with rifle within reach, we wait for the shells to fall in our small corner. We chat and laugh to make the time pass more pleasantly.

I exchange with Reymond a few confidential remarks, justified by the impending danger. Some one on all-fours pulls me by the sleeve. It is Belin, and he wears a most serious look. Belin is no longer our corporal, alas! he was appointed sergeant to the 21st last month.

"Ah! It's you, is it?"

"Well!"

"Listen, I have news for you."

We twist round, and with heads touching one another, Belin continues—

"This is very serious. The captain has just called together the heads of the sections and explained to them the mission on which he is sending our two companies. The engineers are going to destroy with melinite the German barbed-wire; they are to be protected by two patrols of eight men each."

"Well?"

"Then the 21st and the 24th will attack the trench."

"Not a bad programme," remarks Reymond, filling his pipe.

"I don't consider it one bit reasonable," says Belin gravely. "We shall all be demolished."

Silence. Reymond lights his pipe, his head buried in the lap of my coat, so that the flash from his flint may not be seen.

"I came straight away to warn you," adds Belin.

"Very good of you, old fellow, to think of us. But what can we do in the matter?"

"Nothing at all."

"Shall we tell the others?"

"No, indeed! I mentioned the matter to you because you are old friends. But you must not utter a word to the rest; it would only make them uneasy."

This reflection on the part of the sly old fellow makes us quite proud. A grasp of the hand in the dark, a muttered word of thanks, and Belin glides away as noiselessly as he came.

"Maxence, Verrier!" we call out softly.

"What is it?"

"Come here!"

On their approach we give them the news. They merit such confidence just as much as we do.

Then we await the order to attack. Unless.... For, after all, what is an order? We used to discuss the point with Roberty. It is what immediately precedes a counter-order.

And, as a matter of fact, the order is countermanded. It is half-past ten.

The company is put in reserve; swallowed up in a quarry, somewhat similar to our usual grotto, though the entrance is dangerous.

We gain access to it along a narrow passage, very slippery, steep and winding; a sort of toboggan covered with pebbles.

A candle, quick! We gather round the flame.

"Boys," says Reymond, "since we are not going to die immediately, suppose we break into my best *pâté de foie gras*?"

Agreed unanimously. We summon Varlet and Jacquard, and the six of us devour some famous sandwiches. Unfortunately, there is nothing to drink.

And now to sleep. We unfasten the bed-covers and extinguish the candle. It is midnight.

Five minutes afterwards, alarm! Everybody is on his feet. The attack is to take place at dawn. We silently leave the grotto. The two patrols whose duty it is to crawl to the enemy's barbed-wire are appointed. They start, escorted by engineers, who carry large white petards nailed to planks.

The section penetrates into a broad, deep branch, dug by the English a month ago. Endless zigzags. Finally we reach a path lined with lofty poplars. It is pitch-dark and very cold. We tumble into holes, and feel about for corners where we may sit down and take a moment's breath. The ground is covered with frozen mud. Where are we? Where is the enemy?

An order is whispered round—

"When you hear an explosion, you must jump out of the trench and run forward as fast as you can. Pass on the order."

We pass it on. What is most troublesome in an attack is the waiting part. I sit down against a tree and lean on my haversack, which I do not remove. My feet are in a hole. Maxime and I press against each other for support and warmth. We fall into a deep sleep. Another Sunday wasted!

Monday, 9th November.

We awake at dawn and rub our eyes. Well! What of the attack?

"There has been no attack without us," says Maxence.

It has not taken place, after all. The adjutant at the head of the patrol recognized the impossibility of reaching the German wires unseen. Belin was right; the programme could not be realized.... We must try something else.

We find ourselves in a ravine close to the road leading to Maubeuge; in front is a field of beetroots, lying amongst which are the bodies of two Zouaves. The ravine has been converted into a trench by the English, who have constructed here and there little straw-thatched huts. Though the rain has stopped, we splash about in the mud; the mist is icy-cold. We try to keep out the cold with mufflers, gloves, *passe-montagne*; but—how are we to warm our poor feet? It is useless to stamp the soles of our boots on the ground, or knock them against the trunk of a tree. The soup reaches us in a congealed condition.

At three o'clock the infantry come to replace us. Gladly do we give way to them, and the company retires to Bucy. We sleep at "La Rémoise," a combined café and grocer's store. The mistress agrees to serve dinner and allows us to sleep under the tables of the large dining-room, on the floor. Quite enough to satisfy us this evening.

Tuesday, 10th November.

At "La Rémoise" we do not feel at home; we must find something better. On the other side of the street is a house intact. There I find two old people, brother and sister, and after a little bargaining they consent to receive Maxime, Verrier, Reymond, myself, and Jules, for Roberty's former orderly will not leave us. I go off to inform my mates that I have found a lodging-place.

"Bring all your belongings, I have found a *ratayon* and a *ratayonne* willing to provide us with meals and sleeping accommodation."

In the dialect of Soisson, a *ratayon* is an ancestor.

The house is all on the ground-floor, and is entered by five stone steps. Two windows and the door in the middle. The kitchen is in a small building to the right.

Our hosts sleep on mattresses in the cellar. They leave us the two main rooms, and light a small stove which speedily warms the place.

The brother shows me a shell from a 210 gun, and splinters of the same calibre. These he has placed on the window-sill, a place where one would expect to see a petunia.

"I picked up these dirty things in the yard," he explains.

The sister asks us what we do as civilians. Reymond is a painter, to confess which somewhat worries the old dame. But Maxence is a landed proprietor, and Verrier a government official....

"I see you are respectable young men," she remarks. "And so I will fry you some potatoes."

"A good idea, but would you mind—though we don't insist on this—frying a pailful of them?"

"Very well, and for dinner I will stew a rabbit."

Excellent. We brush our coats and give ourselves a good wash with hot water. We spend the whole day in the neighbourhood of the stove, and taste the full delight of being warm and clean.

At twilight the *ratayonne* brings in an oil-lamp. What a nice pleasant thing an oil-lamp is! It immediately fills one with a sense of intimacy and quiet.

The old lady enters with a pot of boiling tea. She sets a bowl before each of us, brings small teaspoons and powdered sugar, and adds—

"The rabbit will be ready at half-past seven. It is a fine plump one."

We chat away. The war news is good.

"Everything seems to point to peace before long. The whole of Europe will be exhausted within three months from now."

Such are the declarations I do not hesitate to utter. The rest nod their heads in approval. Verrier, however, is by nature an enemy to all joy, and so he adds—

"Then you were making a fool of me when you told me at Fontenoy that the war would last a couple of years! What true prophets you are!"

A great roar of laughter silences him.

"Better prophesy," says another, "the possible departure of the 352nd for a town in the centre. This is looked upon as certain, and it would suit me splendidly."

"If only we could get away from the roar of the guns for a fortnight!"

"Don't be too full of self-pity; life is worth living to-night, at all events."

And indeed our refuge seems the very abode of peace and quiet.

The door opens noisily, and Varlet, a short, bearded man, smoking a thick pipe, shouts out—

"We are going back to the trenches."

We all exclaim—

"No, no! We have heard that tale already; you told it us the day before yesterday."

"Well," jeers Varlet, "it wasn't a joke then, and to-night it's a serious matter. Muster in twenty minutes. Get ready."

Thereupon we make a rush to our haversacks. Everything is scattered about: boots and suspenders, bed-clothes and tins of preserves. Everybody speaks at once.

"You're taking my belongings!"

"Look a little more carefully. Surely I know my own business!"

"We shall meet again in the trenches."

A couple of hours will surely be insufficient to restore order out of such chaos. All the same, twenty minutes after the arrival of the messenger of woe, we have re-joined the section, fully armed and equipped, perspiring and out of breath, though not forgetting a single pin.

Our hosts are at the door. The old dame is heartbroken. She keeps repeating—

"You cannot go without dinner, you poor creatures! What of my rabbit? Since you have paid for it, take it with you. Are you going away on an empty stomach?"

"We cannot help it! Such are the horrors of war!"

We glance round the little house and take our departure, somewhat angrily, though we pass it off as though some one had played us a practical joke.

We muster in the dark.

"Number off in fours!"

Each man barks out his number. Then comes the command—

"Right wheel! Quick march!"

"Where are we going, sergeant?"

"Back to the grotto, to spend the night."

And to think of our poor stew! I now understand why the word "rabbit" is sometimes used to express a rendez-vous which comes to nothing.

Wednesday, 11th November.

Distribution of tent canvas to each man. At three o'clock the company mounts to the outposts. Verrier, who has been unwell for some days past, remains in the grotto. It rains the first part of the night.

In the first-line trenches there is no cover: two upright walls of mud. We sit on the ground when we are tired. Maxence says—

"Fling a cover over my head, so that I may smoke a cigarette without being seen."

Not a shot fired to-day.

Thursday, 12th November.

A fine, cold day. The morning mist clears away. Absolute calm. At eight o'clock the cooks, fully equipped and with rifles slung across their shoulders, bring in the soup. A bad sign. They say—

"The company attacks at a quarter-past ten."

"Ah! Good!"

The chiefs of the section confirm the news. The men whistle in a tone that is full of meaning. This time it seems to be serious.

Charensac, a big fellow, is particularly lively. Though no longer a cook, he is in possession of the latest news.

"General attack along the whole front," he explains.

Then he gives forth one of his war-cries—

"Oh dis! Oh dis! Oh dis! Oh dis!"

Charensac is fond of uttering cries devoid of meaning.

We walk to and fro in the trench. The artillery are preparing the attack, and the shells shriek past overhead. The enemy makes no reply. What a din! Impossible to think at all.

Verrier, who, acknowledged to be ill, had remained in the grotto all yesterday, comes rushing up, perspiring and out of breath.

"What are you doing here? This is not the time——"

"It is not the time to leave one's mates," he replies.

He seats himself on the ground and waits.

"Suppose we open a few tins of food," remarks Reymond. "I feel terribly hungry."

Reymond is always ready for a bite or a sup. Nor is he ever downhearted. The acceptance of the inevitable forms part of his hygiene.

We eat, standing, a piece of tunny with our fingers, after cutting slices of bread which serve as plates. Impossible to exchange a dozen words. The explosions of the 75's double in intensity. The roar is deafening.

Quarter-past ten. Forward. The fourth section leaves the trenches. The fusillade gives out a ripping sound with almost brutal effect. The first section, our own, proceeds one by one into a branch, which gradually becomes less deep, and finally runs out on to the open ground. The bullets whistle past. We run ahead with bent bodies, one hand clutching the rifle, the other preventing the bayonet sheath from beating against the leg. It is our business to reach what seems part of a trench a hundred yards ahead, where we shall find temporary shelter.

Verrier stumbles. The thought comes to me—

"There! He's hit!"

Running up to him, I call out—

"Wounded?"

He makes a vague sign indicating that he is not hurt, but points to his panting breast. He has no more breath left.

Here is the trench, into which we leap. Now the bullets pass over our heads.

Reymond is by my side. The spurt has put us out of breath also. We smile at each other.

"Things are serious this morning, eh?"

"I should think so!"

The firing becomes more intense. Some one in front cries—

"Maman!"

We all give a start and look at each other. Who is the man who uttered that shriek of distress?

We hear some one say—

"It's Mignard. He is killed."

From eight to ten men of the section engaged crawl towards us, groaning and moaning.

Little Ramel is amongst them, but he says not a word. His face is perfectly calm as he advances on all-fours.

"What's the matter with you, Ramel?"

"A ball in the abdomen."

We check our impulse to exclaim *"Diable!"* and help him to come down into the trench without shaking him. Poor Ramel, the life and soul of his squadron! He talks quietly to his comrades, and dies in the course of the night.

Another has been hit a fraction of an inch from his eye; the bullet has ploughed his cheek and passed out near the cerebellum. A circuit. He walks sturdily along, and calls out to us—

"Don't I look pretty?"

We hardly dare look at him, the sight is so frightful. One entire half of his face is streaming with blood, the other half is laughing. Evidently the poor fellow has not begun to suffer yet, for he remarks blusteringly—

"This isn't the time to ogle the ladies, is it?" And he points to his torn eye.

Corporal Buche also drags himself along, making signs that he is in pain. Through shot and shell his moans reach us.

Poor Buche! When we crossed Paris, as we came from the depot, he sent for his wife. Mad with joy, she arrived at the Gare Saint-Lazare, and, in spite of the rush and tumult, immediately found her man. And how she kissed and embraced him! It lasted half an hour, without a word being spoken. From time to time they stopped to gaze into each other's eyes at arm's length. Then the kissing began again.

Finally Madame Buche raised her face towards us and declared stoutly—

"We were married on the 1st of August, 1914. I suppose you think this very droll?"

"Not at all!"

Certainly it is anything but droll now to see Buche wounded, tortured by pain. Jestingly we had said to his wife—

"Don't take it so much to heart, Madame Buche; he's sure to come back, you love him so well."

He comes right up to us, and we question him—

"Is it a bad wound?"

"I should think so. My elbow's completely shattered. It hurts abominably."

"Only your elbow? Lucky fellow! We were beginning to be afraid it might be serious."

"What! Isn't it enough?"

"Off you go now, old man. You have played and won; there's nothing more you can do here."

His thoughts fly to his wife, and he sighs—

"We were so gay and lively at the Gare Saint-Lazare!"

"You must tell us about it to-morrow. What are you complaining of when you'll soon be on your way to see her again?"

Each one of us thinks—

"I should be quite content to escape as cheaply as Buche has done."

Naturally those badly wounded say very little, even when they succeed in reaching us.

The order comes to advance towards another trench we can just make out, even farther forward. Lying flat amongst the beetroots, we crawl along like serpents. No one is either gay or sad or over-excited even. Maxence, a huge fellow, is the only one who proceeds on all-fours.

Reymond growls out—

"The megatherium! He'll get himself killed!"

Bullets strike the ground all about us. I can think of nothing but my haversack and *musette*, my can and bayonet sheath which will insist on slipping between my legs. The ground is soft and slimy. I do my best to keep the barrel of my rifle clean. Take care the cartridge cases don't fly open! Crawling along in this fashion is no sinecure. Smoking distracts me, and so I keep my pipe between my teeth. My nose is almost poking into Reymond's heels. From his coat pocket slips a sketch-book. Recognizing its mauve cover, I pick it up, the result being that I am more embarrassed than ever in my anxiety not to lose it.

Reymond descends head foremost into a hole. I follow him.

"Look out, there's some one dead here."

"Take your sketch-book. You dropped it just now."

Evidently he is unnerved, for he answers—

"What the deuce do you expect me to do with that? You might have left it where it was."

The ungrateful fellow!

A few comrades join us. We crowd as well as we can into the trench, taking care not to tread upon the dead body.

The lieutenant in command of the company has walked across the open space which, at his orders, the men have had to crawl across. He now appears before us, safe and sound.

"Who is dead over there?" he asks.

"Mignard has had his brains blown away, *mon lieutenant*. A ball right in the forehead, just as he was scaling the parapet."

Mignard's haversack is unbuckled. His cover is unrolled and wrapped round his head.

More wounded men returning. Here comes one groaning more loudly than the rest. A bullet has pierced his arm above the wrist. He grins as he shakes his injured paw.

"What's the matter with you?"

"I'm certain my arm's broken."

"Move your fingers."

He lifts them up and down like a pianist.

"That will be nothing at all. Shall I dress it for you?"

I cut the sleeve of his coat and shirt. The wound consists of two tiny holes of reddish-brown, one the entrance, the other the exit of the bullet.

"Just a little iodine on it?"

Scared out of his wits, the other says—

"No, no; it would burn too much!"

I dress the wound, and when it is finished say to him—

"Off you go, old fellow; either return to the front or go back to the rear, as you please."

He chooses the rear. Another who has done his day's work.

Reserve squadrons come up. Jouin runs along at full speed instead of crawling. The lieutenant, perceiving him, shouts out—

"Down with you! Down!"

Jouin either does not or will not hear.

"Hear him laughing, the idiot!" remarks the lieutenant, quite furious.

Jouin is at the edge of the trench. One more leap and he will be safe. Just then he stops, looks fixedly at his hand, and falls to the ground. Parvis, his mate and friend from childhood, rushes up to him and says, after a moment's examination—

"He has a couple of bullets right in his chest. Nothing to be done."

"Well, then, come down; it will be your turn next."

"No, I must stay; he is still breathing."

A continuous and indefinable sound, like the gurgle of a bottle being emptied.... It is Jouin in his death agony, which lasts fully a quarter of an hour. Parvis holds his friend's hand, watches his face pale and his features become rigid. He seems not to hear the bullets whistling about his ears.

At last he leaps into the trench, remarking—

"He is dead."

Then, with a shrug of the shoulders, he adds—

"His own fault, idiot as he was!"

Parvis does not understand the meaning of a funeral oration.

A straggler comes creeping up through the beetroots.

"A little more quickly!" exclaims the lieutenant. "Do you want me to come and fetch you?"

The man makes a sign that he is utterly exhausted.

"Are you wounded?"

He shakes his head, indicating that he is not.

Reymond looks at him.

"Why! It's Verrier! Poor old fellow!"

It is indeed Verrier, whose one thought has been all along to join his friends. His strength, however, betrays him, and he lies there flat on the ground.

The lieutenant understands—

"You'd better return, Verrier. I must send you back to the grotto."

A voice answers, as though from a distance—

"Ah! Thanks! Thanks!"

And he quietly returns, exposed to the enemy's fire all the way. I look back after him, and when he makes too long a pause, I remark—

"It's all over. Verrier's dead."

I am mistaken, however, for he soon resumes his crawl. Finally he disappears.

What time is it? Half-past one. How slowly the hours pass!

Two sections of the company are stopped in the open, close to our trench, by deliberately aimed infantry firing.

A lieutenant makes a sign to Sergeant Chaboy, who comes up—

"Take your half-section and bear away to the right of the sections now in action. When you are on a level with them, open fire and hang on to the ground you take."

Another crawl through the beetroots. A fine sport. Without the loss of a man, Chaboy deploys his two squadrons. Some fire whilst others are digging holes. There is only one spade for each squadron, but we scratch away with knives and hands. Very soon we have before us a pile of earth sufficiently high to stop the bullets.

The sergeant sends Jacquard to inform the lieutenant that his orders have been executed. We see Jacquard trot away on all-fours with such agility that, though it is no time for jesting, we cannot refrain from poking fun at him.

"He runs like a rat," says Varlet.

"Or, rather, like a tatou" (an armadillo).

The expression catches on at once. Jacquard returns at a speedy run. His eyes shine, and his complexion is heightened. Before flattening himself on the ground he watches the shells burst, and exclaims in triumph—

"Our projectiles are falling right in the German trenches!"

"Bravo, rat-tatou." (A *ratatouille* is a stew of meat and vegetables.)

The hours pass. Impossible to advance. The fusillade, intense to right and left, slackens in front. Some of the men fall asleep on the spot. Night comes on. The cannonade and the firing almost cease. A cold, clear night and a starry sky. Profound calm. Seven o'clock.

The lieutenant orders our half-section back into the trench. The 24th has been dealt with severely—thirty dead and twenty wounded.

Shall we be relieved to-night? It is sufficiently dark for us to move about behind the trenches and remove the numbness from our limbs.

"Look out, Jouin is there," says Parvis.

It is usual to continue to call the dead by their names.

We form a circle round the body, touch one another on the shoulder and shake hands. We are the more conscious of the value of life from the fact that its tenure in our own bodies is so uncertain.

Mignard, a cover flung over his shattered head, still lies at the bottom of the trench. We shall have to raise him and place him by Jouin's side in the field of beetroots, unless we wish to spend the night with him. He is very heavy. The cold touch of his lifeless hands sends a thrill through my whole body.

But very soon sleep alone occupies our thoughts. The lieutenant remains awake. He looks over the parapet without once removing his eyes. Reymond rolls himself in his cover; I do the same. We throw over our bodies the big poncho, and, close pressed to each other, sleep at the bottom of the trench.

Friday, 13th November.

About two in the morning some one gives me a shake—

"Come along; it's your turn to keep watch over there among the beetroots."

There is a smile on the lieutenant's face as he adds in grumbling accents—

"I never heard any one snore as you do!"

I take up my post, lying flat on the ground, at a distance of fifty yards in front of the trench. I do all I can think of to keep awake. There is a dense mist over the land. After a couple of hours I am relieved. It is raining, of course!

The daybreak is dull and unpleasant. Are we to attack again? No. Yesterday we only had to create a diversion, so the lieutenant explains, and compel the Germans to direct their fire upon our sector. This artillery fire has been sprinkling the plain ever since eight o'clock. The shells shriek overhead and burst away to our left. We remark, jokingly—

"That's nothing; the 21st will catch it all."

During the night a section of the 23rd company, remaining in reserve, has linked up our trench, by means of a branch, with the rear trenches. We are delighted at the idea that we shall no longer have to crawl over exposed country.

The day seems as though it would never end, and nothing happens. Reymond and I, tired out, and seated side by side in a sort of sofa hollowed out in the trench wall, feel not the slightest inclination even to speak. At night the 23rd replaces us and the 24th retires to the grotto.

On reaching it, after forty minutes in the branches, the grotto seems more than ever a paradise to us all.

Each man has his own tale to tell.

Sergeant Moricet shows his coat with a hole right in the middle of the breast; his pocket-book has stopped the bullet, though all the papers in it are cut in pieces.

Corporal Chevalier has been bleeding at the nose ever since the previous evening. At the moment of attack, as he was crawling along, a huge beetroot, hurled forward by a ball, struck him full on the nose. He thought he had swallowed a 210. He now spends all his time in padding his swollen organ.

In the stone bedroom the men are very kind and attentive to one another—

"I hope I'm not in your way, old fellow? Have you enough room to stretch yourself?"

"Yes, thanks. Oh! I beg your pardon if I kicked you."

Each man fusses over the other as though to thank him for not being killed.

The men lie on the ground against their haversacks, their rifles supported against the wall, with cans and all accoutrements hooked on to the guard. The first squadron is complete. Corporal Matois is a big, bearded peasant, from the neighbourhood of Langres, a roughly built countryman. He is really the best character I know.

Charensac, squatting in a corner, is stuffing into his haversack a flannel belt some one has given him. He has already stored away seven shirts, which he intends to carry home with him after the war.

Everything offered him he takes. "Look here, Charensac, would you like this?" Without looking, he shouts out from the other end of the room: "Thanks, old fellow!" It may be what remains at the bottom of a sardine tin, a piece of sausage, chocolate, cigars, a pair of socks, nothing comes amiss. Charensac's stomach is a veritable pit. His haversack, another pit, weighs over sixty-five pounds. Huge shoulders and the flanks of a bull are needed to carry it. He has also two enormous *musettes*, which form baskets projecting on either side. His comrades frequently regard him as a mule. They assure him that he will kill himself. Nothing, however, can rob him of his imperturbable good humour. The only time his face assumes an expression of seriousness is when he affirms: "You should never throw anything away."

Yes, Charensac is quite unique. Never have I seen any one else live through trench warfare with such constant joviality. The men, speaking generally, in spite of their wonderful morale, do not look upon war as a sort of holiday.

Extremely tall and well built, strong as a Turk, a full-moon face enlivened with cunning little eyes, a voice of thunder, a Gargantuan appetite, an ant's rapacity and a dormouse's capacity for sleep, such is Charensac, the gas-fitter from Auvergne. For a packet of canteen tobacco, worth exactly three farthings, you may obtain from him the most extraordinary things, for instance, silence for a space of twenty-four hours. Brawling and uneducated as he is, however, he can count his change quite well, and it is impossible to cheat him. We often say to him: "Charensac, you are nothing but matter!" "Charensac, you make a god of your stomach!" "Charensac, you have every possible vice, you are a disgrace to the first squadron!"

His optimism cannot be shaken by such insults, for he sees in them our inexhaustible goodness of heart.

Henriot coldly looks on at Charensac's evolution. He is a Parisian printer, intelligent and well educated, indifferent to danger, a taciturn fellow, tall and solidly built, almost bald, with the face of a Socrates.

Mauventre, all nose and forehead, always wears a woollen cap, similar to those affected by chestnut sellers. The wretched fellow has a perpetual dread of shells and bullets. Never does the company muster without Mauventre remarking sadly—

"A projectile is bound to drop right in the middle of us."

Briban, a native of Dijon, has a parrot's profile on the body of a shepherd-spider. And finally, Pierrot, nicknamed *"Piaf,"* a Paris drayman, possesses the classic physique of a Zouave.

Piaf and Briban are now our cooks. Briban is called the "Fireman," because, having had his head-gear removed by a bullet in September, after going for a whole week in a cotton cap, he at last found in a field a fireman's *képi*, of which he took immediate possession.

The first company also includes Verrier, Maxence, Varlet, Jacquard, Reymond and myself. A fine squadron.

Sergeant Chaboy enters.

"Have you room for me here?"

We shout out: *"Vive Chaboy!"* and welcome him affectionately, for he has manœuvred his half-section beneath the enemy's fire without losing a single man.

At nine o'clock the lieutenant calls for volunteers to pick up the dead. Varlet, Jacquard, and Charensac offer themselves; they are anxious to bring back two old chums with whom they served before war broke out. They return at midnight.

Saturday, 14th November.

Eight bodies are laid out here, in front of the grotto, with their uniforms all torn and muddy. We try to recognize them.

Around the bodies things follow their ordinary course: fatigue duty, men sweeping and digging the road. The cooks are busy about the fire. Ten men ordered to dig a grave at Bucy cemetery set off, shovel or pick on shoulder.

Belin runs up; he has not been able to get away from his company sooner. On finding us all alive, he lifts his hands in the air and can scarcely contain himself for joy. The 21st has only a few wounded.

We spend the day in relishing the pleasure of being alive; a sensation unknown to civilians.

The relief arrives—a battalion of *Alpins*—and we leave the trenches just as boys leave school on breaking-up day, with feelings of unpolluted joy, and also the thought that the return is in the dim distance and somewhat problematical.

The company is quartered at Acy-le-Haut, where it sojourned in October. At midnight we have to hoist ourselves into a loft by the aid of a ladder, two-thirds of whose rungs are missing. We sink softly into bundles of hay. For twenty-two days, with the exception of two rests of twenty-four hours each at Bucy, we have not left the trenches. Outside it is freezing hard.

CHAPTER IX

A LULL

Sunday, 15th November.

The feelings of utter exhaustion which come over us from time to time do not last long. You think yourself at the last gasp, and yet the following day you are as fresh as possible.

This morning we are taken in charge by Madame Gillot, who lodged us on the 9th October. We receive a warm welcome—

"What, you are all alive!"

Milliard, the postman, brings us over twenty parcels; we are admirably revictualled both in food and in warm clothing.

Monday, 16th November.

Reymond's birthday; he is thirty years of age. To celebrate the occasion, we organize a special lunch.

In the afternoon the lieutenant reviews each man's supplies of food: his haversack, spread open at his feet, must exhibit to the officer's vigilant eye two tins of corned beef, a dozen biscuits, two little bags containing sugar, coffee, and two tablets of condensed soup.

One of our men has neither biscuits nor corned beef. Questioning glance of the lieutenant. Evasive gesture of the man, who immediately stands at attention.

"Have you eaten your two tins of corned beef?"

A sign of assent.

"Your biscuits too, naturally?"

Another sign of assent.

"Ah! And why did you eat your tins of corned beef?"

"*Mon lieutenant*, one evening I was hungry...."

"Better and better! If the men begin to eat their reserve supplies whenever they are hungry, there will be no army left!"

That evening we laughingly relate the incident to Belin. Being an old soldier, he cannot get over it.

"Eat one's reserve supplies without orders! If he had been in the Foreign Legion he would have received eight days' prison for every biscuit missing. The lieutenant was right.... You have your dozen biscuits and two tins, at all events?"

"Of course, don't make such a fuss."

Belin makes a friendly review to assure himself of the fact.

Thin and sharp-featured, his capote well brushed and stretched, and the lower part of his trousers rolled inside his leggings, Belin exhibits subtle poisings of his body and impressive movements of his arm as he points to the sky. He knows how to shout out the "*Hô Mohâmed!*" the rallying cry intended to reach the ears of the comrade who has gone astray.

The ways and manners of civilians in warfare baffle him considerably. Roberty would say to him —

"Strange how much you lack understanding of Parisian humour and fun."

Belin, however, is a brave fellow, he has travelled, read, and fought a great deal. Though we pay him a certain deference, we are very fond of him.

Tuesday, 17th November.

As we are resting we become somewhat like civilians, and await the news with an anxiety unknown at the front, where one's horizon is limited to a field of beetroots.

The papers bring fresh details of the frightful battles of the Yser. The German offensive seems to have been broken. What will they attempt now?

This morning our attack of the 12th is honoured by the following communiqué: "We have made slight progress between Crouy and Vregny." Multum in parvo. Here's something to make us proud, but more especially something to make us modest and patient when we think of what those men are going through who are fighting in the North, living and dying in the thick of it all. It is they who are the real heroes.

From the letters we receive it is manifest that we also are regarded as heroes; people will insist on considering as a gigantic struggle our life as navvies and troglodytes! How absurd! Such lavish use should not be made of these fine expressions, so well deserved by those who have fought at Ypres, Nieuport, and Dixmude.

Here, too, we may deserve them some day. Meanwhile, let us do a little gardening.

Wednesday, 18th November.

We leave Acy to return to the trenches. Madame Gillot stands lamenting at her door.

"Ah! my poor men, I wonder if I shall ever see you again?"

"Very good of you to think of us, Madame Gillot."

The company occupies a new sector in the front line. No dug-outs here, the ground is too hard to do anything. We take sentry duty in the middle of the beet-roots, in a sort of trough dug in the ground, twenty yards in front of the trench. It is snowing.

Thursday, 19th November.

At dawn hoar-frost covers the whole field. A little beyond the barbed wire are three small mounds, covered with snow: the bodies of those of the 24th who died. It is freezing hard, so we stamp our feet on the ground. Red faces emerge from *passe-montagnes*. I carefully press my nose between my woollen-gloved fingers; the sensation of feeling the warmth come gently back is delicious. A few cannon shots from time to time, as though to explain our presence here.

The day is spent in walking as quickly as possible between the two frozen walls of the trench. When I cross Reymond, each of us, before turning round, gravely salutes the other and says: *"Buon di! Buon di!"* like the grotesque doctors in *Monsieur de Pourceaugnac.*

The company, returning to the grotto to sleep, brings back the bodies of eight men, killed on the 12th and picked up between the lines, thanks to the heroism of an auxiliary doctor named Wallon.

Yesterday I received a sleeping-bag made of a kind of soft oil-cloth, lined with flannel: a notable event in a soldier's life. This evening, wrapped in my cover, I enter my sleeping-bag and pull down the edges over my head.

Friday, 20th November.

The trees are now entirely stripped of leaves. The country looks cold and dismal.

The eight bodies are laid out in a line in front of the grotto: the second time we have had such a sight before our eyes. This one is Mallet, who was on guard with us in the train which brought us to the depot. He was a little stout fellow, quiet and taciturn, with a brown beard. War was not at all his vocation, and he would frequently remark with a sigh: "I am certain I shall be killed."

Ill-omened words which should never be spoken.

Mallet wore a medallion on his breast.... The night before the attack he had said quietly to a friend —

"If I die, send this medallion to my wife."

The friend now tenderly unclasps it from his capote. As this latter is being removed from the body, the cloth, covered with frozen mud, is as stiff as cardboard.

After a prolonged examination we recognize Corporal Lion, whose good-natured face has been rendered unrecognizable by a wound. He is another who, speaking of his young wife and children and his past happiness, had imprudently said: "It's all over with me.... I shall never come back!..." There is some difficulty in taking from his shrivelled finger the wedding-ring, the gold of which still shines a little beneath the enveloping mud.

Our nerves are now too hardened for such a sight to affect them. Emotion has become calm and considerate, and each of us thinks—

"Well, if I were in his place, would there be around my body nothing but this cold and gloom of winter?"

The sergeant summons me along with Reymond and Maxence to go on cemetery duty—

"Take a shovel or a pick and go down to Bucy."

In the old cemetery surrounding the church, a lieutenant indicates the spot where we must dig a grave for eight men.

We set to work.

Shortly afterwards a tumbrel brings along the bodies. Two attendants lay them out in a line. Meanwhile, the hole is growing larger. Our shovels encounter old rust-coloured bones, and even an entire skull, which is deposited on the edge of the grave.

At eleven o'clock the work is finished; we return to the grotto for lunch. Above Bucy a duel is being fought between a French and a German aeroplane; the rapid sharp cracks of a *mitrailleuse* reach our ears. Suddenly a jet of flame streams from the German machine, which makes straight for the north, leaving a trail of smoke in its wake. It is hit; the French machine, after circling around, follows after.

On reaching the grotto we learn that the enemy bird fell within our lines on the Maubeuge road. The pilot has succeeded in making good his escape, but our 75's have opened fire upon the machine, which is still burning.

At five in the evening the section is guarding the telephone at Pont-Rouge, on the Bucy road. The light infantry have constructed a hut, which will just hold ten men. Three very comfortable bedsteads, and in one corner a rustic-looking chimney-place, where a magnificent fire sheds its genial warmth. Here we come to roast ourselves in turn, in the intervals of sentry duty.

The cold is bitter; the mud of the beaten track is frozen hard. The roads themselves bristle with clods of frozen earth.

The Pont-Rouge road, which leads direct to the enemy, who is entrenched three hundred yards away, is blocked by a rampart of sand-bags. These bags are covered with blood. It was here that the 5th Battalion, on the 12th of this month, deposited their wounded and dead. A few broken rifles heaped up along the copse, *pêle-mêle* with various military equipment.

Balls whistle in our ears; sometimes they ricochet on the frozen ground and glance off with a singing sound.

Saturday, 21st November.

To-night the thermometer is 13° Centigrade below zero. I have slept very well, in the open air, rolled in canvas wrappings at the bottom of the trench. On waking I see Jacquard's hirsute beard, kind innocent eyes and red nose. The rest of his face is swathed in chestnut-coloured wool. Quick, my bottle and a good mouthful of brandy. Just in time, for the cold has surprised us during the night and frozen me to the very bones. I pick up my can, which I had laid aside during sleep: it is full of icicles. The coffee is frozen.

The cold has brought out a number of fantastic costumes. One of my comrades looks like a bashi-bazouk, another like a chorus singer in *Boris Godounow*. To write a letter I put on great red woollen gloves, a grey muffler, and a blue *passe-montagne*. I also wear trousers of green velvet; the effect being quite good.

All the same, it must not be imagined that we look disguised. At muster, the blue uniform reappears and the usual military aspect of things; we remain soldiers beneath our fantastic accoutrement, having all become so without an effort of will. Adaptation to the drudgery and difficulties of the profession comes about insensibly.

Luckily, the wind is not blowing in the direction of the trench; but the enemy's bullets pour in a raking fire. Maxence, who is extremely tall and too careless to bend down, just misses being killed on two occasions. His calm is most exasperating. We shriek at him—

"*Sale rosse!* I suppose you'll be happy when you've got a bullet through your head. And you think it will be a joke for us to carry you away dead, a giant like you?"

"He weighs at least a hundred and eighty pounds," growls Jacquard, who is a dwarf in comparison.

After all, frost is better than rain and mud.

Sunday, 22nd November.

The squadron's new quarters at Bucy are not very luxurious: an abandoned building, considerably broken up, windows smashed, doors and casements torn away. Along a narrow flight of stairs, we gain access to two square rooms.

Fortunately the people next door are willing to lodge us. Inside the wide street-door is a little yard; to the right, a rabbit-hutch which is empty; to the left, a ground-floor room with cellar and loft. Doubtless the house is protected from enfilade firing, for it has remained standing, though a 77 has made a slight breach in it, above a sign-post on which we read: "Achain, mattress-maker."

We enter, meeting with a cordial reception.

"It's a poor place," says the woman, whose round face is framed in a black shawl, "but we will give you every attention."

Poor, indeed! Nothing of the kind. The windows are unbroken, the roof intact, the doors will shut, and there is a fire in the stove. In a small room a couple of beds and a mattress laid on the floor are to be placed at our disposal.

The owners of the house sleep in the cellar. The consequence is that we are masters for the time being, one of the advantages-perhaps the only one—of the bombardment.

Numbers of parcels arrive. Beneath the stupefied gaze of the Achains, we unpack tins of preserved food, which Jules arranges on a sideboard. Jules explains that we belong to the most refined and select classes of society. It is a mania of his to proclaim everywhere that we are persons of distinction. We make our appearance, tired to death and covered with mud, bundled up in mufflers, with shaggy cadaverous faces, carrying rifles, haversacks, pipes, mud, and making a horrible clatter. Our hosts, troubled by such an invasion, at first manifest a certain degree of reserve, but Jules speedily finds reassuring words; he exhorts us to mend our manners, and pays court to the ladies. A most valuable fellow, Jules!

He is a native of Franche-Comté. Evidently this district does not produce thin sorry-looking specimens of humanity. Jules possesses the frame and physique of a wrestler. His big shining face, flanked with enormous ears, is illumined by two small eyes which give the impression that he may be a very difficult person to deal with.

Jules is a born orderly. He has far more opportunities for exercising his subtlety behind the trenches than on the line; his vocation is to supply us with stores from outside the recognized limits. When on this quest, he fears no one and will go anywhere.

In September he had not been a couple of hours on duty before giving proof of his abilities: he found Roberty's canteen, which had gone astray during the retreat, replenished our store of tobacco, and brought back with him a rabbit, a fowl, three litres of wine and a bottle of spirits.

"You can put this latter into your coffee," he said; "it will then be worth drinking."

On the day we enticed him away, Jules, having lost his lieutenant, had also lost his position as orderly, and forfeiting his privileges occupied a lower position in the ranks. The adjutant, whose offers he had scorned, told him dryly that he would return to the squadron without any position at all. Jules did not like disputes, and pretended to submit to his destiny. He resumed his place in the squadron, though only to occupy himself with our personal affairs, in spite of officials, roll-calls and laws.

The personal affairs of six soldiers in the second class do not seem a very serious matter, especially in such busy times. Still, it took all Jules' activity to attend to them.

"I say, old fellow, we are coming down from the outposts this evening and sleeping in the village. Run along and find us a house."

Jules pretends to be considerably embarrassed. He raises his arms, takes his *képi* between his first finger and thumb, and scratching his head with his other three fingers, says—

"That's just your way! Jules, find me this, or Jules, find me that! This very morning, Jules cut the roll-call to do your messages, and the corporal marked him absent."

"Come! come! not so much talk. We shall be in the village by nightfall. You must get there before us. We rely on you for beds and dinner."

"What if I am caught by the gendarmes? Or suppose I meet the colonel?"

Then we appeal to his vanity—

"You can easily outwit all the gendarmes in the place. And a fellow like you is clever enough to make up some plausible tale that will satisfy the colonel."

An appeal is also made to his interests. Nothing further is needed, and when, five minutes afterwards, some one calls for Jules, he has disappeared.

The lodging is found and dinner in full swing. Jules confides to the company in general—

"At first the mistress refused to lodge six soldiers. But I talked her round. Besides, I gave her to understand that you were real gentlemen."

The natives of the South of France may be braggarts; anyhow, this one from the Franche-Comté could easily give them points. If mention is made of a farmer's wife or even of some lady of the manor within a radius of ten leagues, Jules begins to cluck like a hen, to slap his hands on his thighs, and with appropriate gestures he gives us to understand that he knows the lady in question very well indeed.

In his own district he was attached to a farm, and in his leisure hours he most certainly gave himself up to poaching.

Not on account of the war will he abandon his petty occupations. No, indeed, something must be done to break the monotony of trench life.

From time to time, in spite of gendarmes and regulations, Jules trips over to Soissons. He returns with an entire bazaar in his *musettes*.

"I sell it all again, you know, at cost price," he explains. "There are times when I lose."

"Of course!"

The other day he brought back a small hunting carbine. He also managed to procure the whole paraphernalia required for making snares and traps.

He is away for hours at a time, prowling about the woods, risking a court-martial a score of times, all to bring back a few tom-tits. On his return, blood and feathers are sticking to his fingers.

"You savage!" exclaims Verrier. "Doesn't war provide you with sufficient opportunities to satisfy your bloodthirsty instincts? Why should you go and kill tiny birds like these?"

"Don't cry over it; I am going to cook them for you, along with a few slices of bacon...."

To-day, thanks to Jules, we are *en famille* with the Achains. The little girl, ten years of age, has pretty blue eyes and light hair, confined in a black shawl, like her mother's. She looks at haversacks, rifles, and *musettes*, and asks in drawling accents—

"Do you really carry all these things on your back?"

Indeed, the haversacks do look of a respectable size: on the top the cover, rolled in the sleeping-bag; to the left, a tent canvas; to the right, a rubber mantle; in the middle, a cooking utensil; inside, linen and tobacco, a thread and needle-case, slippers, a large packet of letters, and reserve provisions. The whole weighs nearly thirty-five pounds. The *musettes*, too, are of enormous bulk, swollen with provisions, toilet utensils, a ball of bread, evidently so called because it is flat, spirit-flask, knife, fork, and spoon, a tin plate, and lastly a few packets of cartridges. At the bottom is a confused mass of tobacco and matches, bread-crumbs, and earth.

Sergeant Chaboy announces *en passant*—

"Be ready at five o'clock, my boys. It is the section's turn to act as artillery support at the Montagne farm."

The Germans are beginning to fire upon the village. At four o'clock the bombardment is at its height. Impossible to remain in the streets.

The light begins to fade, and the projectiles become fewer and fewer. The section musters.

The Montagne farm is isolated right in the centre of a plain which overlooks Bucy, and on which several batteries of our 75's have been installed.

Every day the Germans pour showers of projectiles on to the position. This evening their shells set fire to a straw-rick. The flames illumine the whole summit, throw into relief the desolate outlines of the trees, and project their lurid reflections on to the surrounding buildings. We hear the crackling of the straw as the flaming sprays are carried away in the distance. The section slowly advances towards the farm in columns of twos. We halt on reaching a stable, where we find a quantity of thick litter. All the better, for it is bitterly cold; several degrees below zero.

At midnight I am on guard with Reymond in front of the door. It is a clear, starry night. We hide ourselves in a corner against one of the pillars of the doorway, to obtain shelter from the icy north wind. Here we stand for a couple of hours. What is there for us to do? We begin by expressing, as Anatole France says: "most innocent thoughts in most crude terms."

Away in the distance the dull roar of a cannon. The shrieking sound draws nearer.

"Appears as though it were meant for us!"

The shell whirls past and bursts a hundred yards from the door.

A grunt of satisfaction on finding that the explosion has taken place at a safe distance.

One observation: the shrieking of shells almost at the end of their course reminds one of the howl of a dog baying the moon.

Shots follow one another. Every minute the distant "boom," then the hissing sound, which gradually grows more intense, and finally the explosion, a rending crash close at hand, followed by vibrations and the noise of broken branches. Not the slightest refuge for us.

"Not often have I been annoyed as I am this evening," remarks one of us.

"Nor I either!" remarks the other.

"They might have waited till we had finished sentry duty before bombarding us."

Renewed explosions. The door slightly opens, and the head of Corporal Chevalier appears.

"Is the bombardment pretty violent?"

"Bah! Nothing extraordinary."

"The fact is—the lieutenant has sent me to say that, if things begin to look too serious, you may return. Useless to get killed for nothing."

We would gladly have profited by the permission. Chevalier, however, does not belong to our squadron. Consequently we politely reply—

"All right, corporal, our best thanks to the lieutenant. We may as well finish our watch."

Chevalier's head disappears. The door shuts. Fresh shells.

"How stupid of us to swagger in this way!" we reflect.

On coming to relieve us, the two following sentries, after muffling themselves up by lantern light, ask—

"A pretty heavy bombardment just now, eh?"

I have the audacity to reply—

"Ah! We did not even pay attention to it, we were talking."

And so, *"La tempeste finie, Panurge faict le bon compaignon,"* as Rabelais said.

Monday, 23rd November.

The lieutenant appears at the door and calls out—

"Everybody under shelter, to the grottoes. The bombardment is beginning again."

At that moment, indeed, a projectile dashes down upon one of the farm buildings, smashing in the stable roof. To reach the grottoes we have to run a hundred yards through the darkness. We are in the open. Those who have candles light them. *Tableau.* The grotto has been transformed into a sheep-fold. Several hundreds of sheep are moving to and fro, bleating all the time in stupid fashion.

Meanwhile, the German artillery is raining upon the farm and its outhouses. A fowl is killed on a dunghill by a shrapnel ball. What with the boom of the cannon and the bleating of the sheep, the hours pass very slowly. Reymond, however, pilots us over the grotto as though it were a gallery of Roman catacombs. Provided with a piece of candle, he mumbles away like a sexton: *"Questo è la tomba di santa Cecilia; tutto marmo antico!"* When the cannonade stops, out in the yard he organizes a fancy bullfight, in which each of us, supplied with the necessary accessories, in turn impersonates the bull, the espada, the banderillero, the picador, or the disembowelled steed.

We play like schoolboys at recreation time, until we are quite out of breath with laughter and exertion, and then sit down on the very spot around which shells have so recently been falling.

The Prussians have fired forty thousand francs' worth of munitions and have killed a fowl, which, by the way, our own gunners have eaten!

On the section returning to Bucy, the general impression is summed up in the remark—

"After all, it has been rare sport!"

Tuesday, 24th November.

Snow is falling, and so we remain indoors. The postman's visit forms our only distraction. After yesterday's uproar the guns are quiet to-day. No set of men are ever so capricious as gunners. The inhabitants of Bucy, who have spent a day and a night crouching in their cellars, walk about the streets this afternoon as though everything were once more normal. There is little damage done to the streets, since the Germans mainly fired with their 77's.

Wednesday, 25th November.

A lieutenant is chatting at the hospital door with the major. All of a sudden he falls to the ground. We gather round him, and find that he has received a bullet in the abdomen. The street opposite the hospital being perpendicular to the German trenches, spent bullets sometimes take it in enfilade, and an accident happens.

During roll-call, which takes place in the main street, a shrapnel explodes on a neighbouring house. Broken tiles rain down upon us. Instinctively we "form a carapace." The lieutenant has not stirred a muscle. "Surely," he remarks, "you are not going to get excited over a little falling dirt. Attention!" We all line up and stand at attention. The next moment the ranks are broken, and each man returns to his quarters, laughing and joking at the incident.

After all, we make a jest of everything. This is the secret of that dash and enthusiasm boasted of in the official communiqués, and about which civilians must have the most vague ideas. The good humour that has stood a campaign of four months must be in the grain; at all events, it is of quite a special kind.

The source of our morale lies in the fact that we accept life as we find it.

This evening the company returns to the trenches and sleeps in the grotto.

Thursday, 26th November.

The frost has disappeared; now we have a thaw with its inevitable filth and mud. The entrance of the grotto is a veritable sewer. We enter along slippery slopes, almost impassable.

Latest news from the kitchens: the regiment is about to leave for the fort of Arche, near Epinal, unless it goes on to Amiens ... unless, again, it remains here.

This evening, in the grotto, Maxence lies on his back smoking a cigarette. He murmurs softly to Reymond, who is making a sketch, some lines from the *Fêtes galantes*—

> *Au calme clair de lune triste et beau*
> *Qui fait rêver les oiseaux dans les arbres*
> *Et sangloter d'extase les jets d'eau,*
> *Les grands jets d'eau sveltes parmi les marbres.*

Varlet, naked down to the waist, turns round and round, rolling himself in his flannel girdle, one end of which is held tight by Meuret, who is always ready to lend a helping hand. Mauventre, *Piaf*, and the "Fireman" are playing cards with the corporal, making comments on each move. Charensac crouches down, drawing up an inventory of the wealth he has stored away in his haversack. The rest, rolled snugly in their coverings, sleep and snore.

Friday, 27th November.

Our artillery vigorously bombards the enemy's trenches. Nothing to do except watch the shells—and the rain—fall.

Saturday, 28th November.

In the front line the section occupies a new sector, not yet completed. A misty maddening rain chills us to the very bones. Impossible to see twenty yards in front of one. The kind of weather which gives you the impression that the sun has left this world and will never return.

Sunday, 29th November.

The 24th goes down to Bucy at six in the evening.

Our hosts know the hour we are to be relieved. They expect us.

"*Sainte Vierge*, what a filthy condition you are in!" exclaims Madame Achain.

We are delighted to see our beds once again. Madame Achain would gladly change the bed linen, if she had any—but she has not, and one must not be too dainty in war time.

Monday, 30th November.

Another quiet day spent by the fireside in conversation, playing cards and writing letters.

This morning Jacquard is charged with the making of our chocolate. When the six bowls, filled to the brim, are on the table, he calls out—

"Come, messieurs, breakfast is waiting, messieurs!"

How grandiloquent it sounds!

We appear, only half awake, slouching along in slippers and old shoes. If perchance the chocolate is boiled too much or too little, if it is too thick or too thin, then the patient Jacquard must submit to sarcastic reproaches, to complaints from men who, most assuredly, would not tolerate the slightest inconvenience!

Tuesday, 1st December.

To-day we are road-labourers, an occupation lacking interest, though preferable to that of grave-digger.

The section has been ordered to clean the Pont-Rouge road, in anticipation of the visit of the general. We start with shovels and brooms on our shoulders. Luckily, it is not raining. The Pont-Rouge road is filthy; that, however, is its slightest defect: it is also infested with projectiles. We are not enthusiastic about the work. No one is wounded.

Wednesday, 2nd; Thursday, 3rd December.

At eight o'clock the company musters in a farmyard, proceeding to a field north of Bucy for drill. The soil is ploughed by huge shells which daily continue to fall. Fortunately they have so far chosen a different hour from ours, thus avoiding unpleasant encounters. Here we have section school: "Count off in fours! Right wheel! Line up! Shoulder arms! Right! Left turn!—Left!"

The men manœuvre in very lethargic fashion. Even the words of command have no life in them. The sergeant shouts out—

"Right-about turn!—Right!"

He adds—

"This isn't a march at all, it's a paddle!"

Towards the end of the drill we deploy in skirmish line, and fling ourselves on our knees before a hail of imaginary bullets.

"Let each man practise the right position for charging. Fire three cartridges at the enemy debouching at the outskirts of the wood. Three hundred yards—Fire!"

The lieutenant pleads with us—

"Come, come, if you will drill well for five minutes I will march you back to quarters."

It is the greatest mistake in the world to drill without putting one's heart into it. As Belin emphatically says—

"Troops that cannot do manual exercises are no better than a flock of sheep."

And the rascal is right, too, as he always is.

Friday, 4th December.

At night the company musters to mount to the trenches. On the right, for a few hundred yards, we proceed along the side of the wood, whilst to the left stretches an endless field of beetroots, in the midst of which the Germans are entrenched. In this field has been dug the branch leading to the first line. It is completely dark, and the ground is quite soft; the twenty-five minutes' crossing of this branch is a most disagreeable piece of work. We knock against all sorts of corners, slip about, and fall against the slimy walls.

Passages open out from time to time; these are second-line trenches, or else branches connecting together the various sectors. Moreover, first- and second-line trenches resemble the branches, though somewhat wider and provided with earthen parapets in the direction of the enemy.

We are all on duty until nine o'clock. The Germans fire their rifles to inform us that they are there. We blaze away in their direction for the same reason.

About ten everything is calm. It is raining. Earth and sky seem blended in one general flood.

Varlet, with his hood, looks like a dwarf out of some book of fairy tales; Jacquard wears a knitted helmet, out of which emerges a fan-shaped beard; he covers his shoulders with an oil-cloth stole. He looks like a chorister masquerading as a crusader. Reymond, draped in a huge khaki poncho, might have been a member of the Holy League.

The walls of the trench are slippery and fall in. There are but few dug-outs, scarcely any of which can be used because of the water finding its way through the badly jointed planks. The only possible shelter consists of kennels made on the surface of the ground, into which a man may coil himself. Take care, however, lest they fall in!

We can do nothing but submit to the rain, and let ourselves be submerged. This is no longer war, it's a deluge.

Saturday, 5th December.

Everybody must be up on watch duty before dawn. This is the regulation hour for counter-attacks.... As a rule it is the quietest time of the day. About seven the cooks bring coffee and letters. After swallowing the one and devouring the others, there remains but little to do; we doze about, play cards, perhaps, in case we find a sufficiently dry spot. Or we may be sent off on a cleaning expedition, scraping the mud away from the floor of the branch trench.

About noon the cooks appear again—

"Lunch-time!"

There are two of them—*Piaf* and the "Fireman" in shirt-sleeves—one carrying the dish full of meat, the other carrying the two big vessels containing respectively soup and coffee.

They fill our plates and *gamelles*. Our hands are caked with earth. The "Fireman" pours out for each man a little of the mess alcohol—a nasty mixture containing tincture of iodine; we swallow it like whey. Frequently there is wine to drink. We drag out the meal to kill time.

From half-past three onwards we are very impatient. We shall not be relieved before nightfall. By reason of the narrowness of branches and trenches it becomes most difficult to make room for the new arrivals. They can pass along only when we squeeze ourselves into a corner, like herrings in a barrel. To-night the company is not going down into the grotto; it must occupy another emplacement, also in the front line.

Appearance of a German engine which we immediately nickname the "torpedo"—a formidable explosion preceded by no hissing sound whatsoever; a blinding flash, prolonged vibrations, projectiles flung in every direction. At first we are somewhat stupefied. As I am carrying an order from the lieutenant to the adjutant, a torpedo explodes on the parapet, lifts a couple of men off their feet and covers me with earth. No one is hurt. This new invention seems to make more noise than it does injury—on condition, of course, that the projectile does not come down direct on the trench itself.

Sunday, 6th December.

This morning the sun is shining! How pleasant not to have one's head bowed and one's back bent before the storm! Several days of incessant rain have transformed the trenches into streams of mud. We sink over our ankles in a slimy, yellowish cream. Third night in the first line.

Monday, 7th December.

We are relieved at five in the afternoon. We run through the branches in all the greater hurry because we are going to our quarters. Every dozen steps we slip or stumble.

I managed to reach the Achains' before the rest to order dinner. On the threshold I have to answer the invariable question: "No one missing?" I reply gaily—

"Of course not, but we are all very dirty and tired, and as hungry as wolves."

After removing our trappings and leaning our rifles in a corner, whilst awaiting the arrival of our friends, we relate the paltry happenings of the last four days: the dark nights and heavy rainfall, the skirmishes, the bombardment, etc.

"And what of you here, has much damage been caused?"

The fact is that our village is being shelled almost daily, but the inhabitants scarcely pay attention to it. They have acquired somewhat of our mentality as soldiers, just as we have adopted something of their peasant nature. They know that in war one must be astonished at nothing.

No, this time no great damage has been done.

"A 150 shell exploded in Madame B.'s garden, over there on the right, and *père* Untel just missed being killed in his loft by a spent ball."

We remark gravely—

"All the same, things look bad."

We shake our heads just as old fogies do when the crops are likely to prove a failure.

One old dame asks anxiously—

"At all events, you'll not let them come back here?"

At this moment our comrades burst in, Jacquard at the head, haversack on back, pipe in mouth, muddy and all muffled up. His big face, with its shaggy beard, beams with goodwill. He brandishes his big rifle in his small arms and thunders forth—

"Let them come back! No indeed, my good woman; they'd have to pass over our bodies first!"

We approve of what he says, and succeed in calming him down.

The mistress, an optimist, declares in her country accent—

"Shall I tell you what I think?"

"Certainly."

"Well, then, some fine day they will clear off without any one suspecting it."

"*Mon Dieu*, for my part, I shouldn't object if— —"

Our existence is now as well regulated as that of any Government official: four days in the trenches, four days at Bucy, four days in the trenches, and so on.

How glad we are to get back to the house and our old habits!

Yes, we keep to these habits, though they are far different from those we followed in the bygone days of peace. It may be that we do so because we know them to be so fragile and uncertain, like ourselves, and at the mercy of the least of the hazards of war.

After dinner, then, one game of cards, two, three. Some other game as an occasional novelty, though we always return to the noble game of manilla.

Milliard goes from house to house with the letters for each squadron. Here he comes. A sound of footsteps in the yard. We raise our heads; is it he? It is. He knocks on the window-pane. We all spring to the door. The postman is welcomed as eagerly as though he were the bearer of victory and peace. He draws up to the lamp, reads the envelopes, and sits down. If there are but few letters he apologizes.

Henriot and he chatter away by the fireside for a few minutes.

"Come, boys, quick, give me your letters," says Milliard. "I have three more squadrons to serve."

Our thanks follow him right into the yard.

To bed early this evening.

Tuesday, 8th December.

We do the best we can to clean our clothes. A knife has to be used for scraping coats and puttees, to which great scales of mud are sticking. Disputes burst out. Who is the first for the hand-basin?

Some such remark as the following is heard—

"You're not going to keep it all to yourself, as you did last time, I suppose?"

The charge of selfishness is the one most frequently hurled at another man's head.

"You make use of it yourself first," says one man, "and then you think of others."

"Well, and what of yourself? Yesterday you refused me a bar of chocolate, because of the trouble it would have given you to unfasten your haversack."

"And you, the other day when preparing mess, didn't you go away and leave me to carry a huge pail all alone? Did you, or did you not?"

Such is the conversation of heroes!

The whole of the first day in quarters is spent in cleaning. At night all six of us appear shaven and brushed, combed and washed, and the *far niente* begins. A feeling of boredom comes over us. There is nothing to remind us that we are at war, none of war's accoutrements, at all events. Reymond has adopted a colourist's costume to rest in: a black and yellow streaked cap, a short green woollen jacket, blue cloth trousers, grey gaiters, a violet girdle from which hangs a broad knife in its sheath, a red and white-specked tobacco-pouch, and a long wick of orange-coloured tinder. The effect seems to him harmonious, and the lieutenant who happened to pass along and dropped in a few minutes ago appeared delighted and somewhat surprised.

The rest content themselves with a more sober get-up, though just as little military in style: blue cloth or chestnut velvet trousers, slippers, and frequently a woollen cap.

Nothing happens of a nature to enliven our existence. Drill in the morning, but this is something it is impossible to "cut."

Between meals I write letters. Maxence, seated near the fire, with his legs crossed and his hand under his chin, smokes cigarettes. He muses, and at the same time keeps an eye on a rice pudding on the point of boiling over. This native of Franche-Comté feasts on the most insipid things, and obstinately refuses to drink wine or to eat cheese. Fond of hunting, he chatters away to Jules, who comes from the same province. Landed proprietor and poacher discuss the different methods of tracking a hare, and talk seriously about other matters connected with hunting. In a corner Varlet reads everything he can lay his hands on, even old illustrated journals. Sometimes he starts off on an expedition and brings back a leg of mutton. Jacquard, a jack-of-all-trades, is always doing something, either cooking or repairing. Verrier, our treasurer, slowly and minutely brings the accounts up to date, with the gravity and seriousness he bestows on everything he undertakes. Simply watching him roll a cigarette enables one to see that he never does anything lightly.

About noon the *Petit Parisien* reaches Bucy. The reading of the communiqué and the dispatches gives us to understand how impossible it is to foresee the end of the war. Six months ... a year.... Such are the hypotheses we once laughed at, though now they appear logical enough. At bottom, we believe there will happen something unexpected and formidable which will bring victory and peace....

Then we begin to discuss matters. Since all six of us are bound by the ties of true friendship, there is nothing upon which we are of one mind: Varlet, a working electrician, who has often found it difficult to make ends meet, considers that everything is not for the best in the best of all societies. Maxence, with a stake in the land, regards Varlet as a dangerous customer. Jacquard, who is in the hosiery business, is a well-balanced individual, very optimistic, who reads between the lines of every dispatch the coming entry of the Russians into Berlin, and the complete exhaustion of Germany. Verrier is a moderate and restrained sort of fellow. He says: "I am just going to sleep a little," or "eat a little," or "wash myself a little." Always "a little." We call him: "not too much," or sometimes *Verrierus tristis*, the silent. He forms an interesting contrast to the exuberant Reymond.

Mother Achain and her little daughter, their heads enveloped in black kerchiefs and their hands clasped on their knees, smile quietly as they watch us bawl and gesticulate. Father Achain, in the darkest recess of the room, between fireplace and bed, is everlastingly drawing away at a pipe that has gone out. From time to time he walks to the door and stands there for a while. On returning, he says—

"There's some heavy firing going on above the Gué-Brûlé."

Saturday, 12th December.

Bad news from Russia....

At six in the evening we return to the trenches. Whilst marching along, our company crosses some light infantry.

"Hullo!" they say, "here come the foot-soldiers."

And what scorn they would convey by the word "foot-soldiers!"

Well, and what are they themselves, after all?

Sunday, 13th December.

The whole day is spent in the grotto. It rains so heavily that fatigue duty is suppressed. We are all either sitting or sprawling on the ground, engaged in reading, writing, or eating by the light of a few candles. A practical joke, repeated again and again, and of which we never tire, consists in taking aim at some one intently reading a letter or a book, and hurling at his candle a shoe, a loaf, or a *gamelle*. Sometimes a nose is hit instead of the candle. Thereupon huge guffaws ensue. Varlet, who considers that I am in a sad mood this evening, cannot resist the temptation of taking me by the feet and dragging me on my back three times round the room. I laugh heartily. Then we both crawl about on all-fours, look in the chopped straw for my pipe, tobacco-pouch, knife, and the small change that has dropped from my pocket.

Another distraction: we have to carry from the grotto to the first-line trenches great rolls of barbed wire, as wide as a barrel and several yards in length. The things are most difficult to handle. On reaching the outposts, we hoist them over the parapet.

Henriot and Milliard, having fastened up the letters and parcels in bags, place these bags on to a barrow and mount to the trenches. The ascent is steep, and the barrow sticks in the mud. From afar we see our two friends climbing the hill. Some one shouts out—

"Letters!"

Thereupon there is a rush in the direction of the postman. A dozen men are now wheeling the barrow along. Then come the questions—

"Is there a letter for me? Tell me if my parcel has arrived?"

If the answer is in the affirmative—

"Quick, give it to me; hurry up!"

Then the distribution takes place very speedily, for Milliard never gets in a temper. We enter the grotto, and at the foot of one of the great pillars supporting the vault Milliard attends to his business. His silhouette and those of the men around show up black against the background of light formed by the opening of the grotto. A dismal-looking tree, standing on a rising ground, exhibits its leafless branches.

When the weather is fine the distribution takes place outside skirting the wood, whose leaves we have seen first turn yellow and then fall to the ground....

Milliard says—

"Don't crowd around; you shall all be served in turn!"

We group around him.

"Now for the parcels!" Milliard calls out the names.

"Present! Here!"

The parcel flies above our heads in the direction of the answer.

Monday, 14th December.

We are now in the first line, sometimes keeping a watch over the field of beet-roots, sometimes, pick or shovel in hand, digging and clearing away.

The entire plain is furrowed with a vast network of fortifications. The Germans construct listening posts eighty yards distant from our own. In a few more weeks the wires will be touching one another.

From our front lines project antennæ or feelers, portions of trench driven as near as possible to the enemy, and connected with the main trench by a deep zig-zag branch.

For sheltering purposes we build small huts somewhat resembling those in which the bodies were deposited in the catacombs. Here the men keep themselves dry, at all events. A couple of tent canvasses unfolded in front of the opening are a protection from the cold, and enable one to light a candle without making oneself a target for the enemy.

During the night, over a sector of one kilometre, there are fired on an average a thousand rifle shots which neither kill nor wound a single man. The object of this fusillade is simply to prevent the patrols from moving to and fro between the lines.

Tuesday, 15th December.

For some days past I have been feeling shaky. Really I shall have to go to the hospital. The day sergeant passes through the trenches and calls out—

"Any one ill to-day?"

"Yes, I am."

He writes down my name.

"Is that all? Come, now, there must be some one else. Is any one tired belonging to the 24th?"

He goes from squadron to squadron picking up those who are sick.

Five *poilus* give themselves up. As a matter of fact, it is not very pleasant to report yourself ill in the first line. You have first to make your way through the branches, then go down to Bucy along a road that is being bombarded, and finally return to where you started unless the major gives his verdict that you are to be "exempt from trench service."

At the top of the village, alongside a small hill, a temporary hospital has been fitted up in a rather fine-looking house, abandoned by its owners at the time of the offensive of von Kluck. The lawns are ornamented with statues.

In the centre of the yard patients await the hour of the doctor's visit. Few serious cases; chiefly the wan expressions and dejected looks of tired men.

Here comes the major. He has just finished breakfast with the colonel, who is staying at the château opposite. He is from the Vosges—young-looking and slim, average height, of ruddy complexion, with a rough voice and dark, piercing eyes. As each man awaits his turn he questions the attendants—

"Is the major in good humour this morning?"

The examination begins. The patients enter in batches of ten. They disrobe in a corner, jostling and being jostled by their neighbours. They run a great risk of never seeing their clothes again, for these latter are deposited along the wall, and speedily become trampled about the floor.

The major sits in front of a table, near the window. He spends half a minute with each man.

Sometimes a man has a variety of ailments. He suffers all over: head and loins, liver and heart and feet.

"Clear out at once!" exclaims the major.

Those who come from rural districts all complain of the stomach, an organ which is just as likely to represent to their minds the bronchi as the intestines. The doctor accordingly asks—

"Which stomach? The one that eats or the one that breathes?"

Every one receives his deserts. The genuine cases are "exempt from trench service"; those who are war-worn and tired out are exempted from some particular duty. As for the rest, the major writes opposite their names on the sergeant's card the words, *Visite motivée,* a cabalistic formula implying that there was no reason whatsoever why they should have come up for examination.

Things are carried on just the same as in barracks; the same tricks are employed. The other day Jules unhesitatingly placed on the stove the thermometer which the attendant had put in his armpit. The mercury rose to 430 Centigrade! The doctor nearly had a fit. Jules is still outside the hospital walls.

At the exit those officially recognized as ill appear with radiant faces; those who have met with a snubbing and are declared to be well have drawn features and generally the air of a man at death's door.

Opposite my name the major has written, "To be kept in hospital." I look as though I had won the first prize in a lottery, and already feel considerably better.

The attendants carry me off to their room, a regular paradise. A 105 shell has fallen right on the staircase, reducing everything to matchwood on its way, but the rest of the place is intact: beds, a large fire, a good table, lamps. We play at cards, smoke, chat, do anything to kill time. Outside, for a change, the rain falls harder than ever.

CHAPTER X

BOMBARDMENTS

Thursday, 17th December.

I leave the hospital and make my way to the Achains' to wait for my five mates, who at nightfall will come down from the trenches with the rest of the company. I lay the cover: heavy plates with pieces broken off, tin forks and spoons, thick glasses. No knives; each man must supply his own.

Here they come at last.... What a state they are in! Mud from head to foot. Quick with their letters, slippers, and something to eat. We stay up late, chatting by the fireside.

Friday, 18th December.

This evening the section is on guard at the Montagne farm, but Reymond, momentarily requisitioned for some design work at the commander's bureau, remains at Bucy; I also stay behind, having just left the hospital.

This Montagne farm is anything but a pleasant spot. Yesterday another light infantryman was carried away with his head shattered by a 150-gun shell.

Our friends start at four. We should be glad to see them back again already.

"Now, be careful. No nonsense, remember!"

A *tête-à-tête* dinner, a very quiet affair, after which we lie down on our beds.

"How comfortable!"

Yes, indeed, this is the real thing. We might almost imagine ourselves back in civil life!

The low-roofed room, which receives air and light only by way of the door, was evidently white-washed long ago. There are spiders' webs in every corner. The floor consists of beaten earth. The walls are bare except for two chromos— Nicholas II and Félix Faure—just visible beneath fly-stained glasses. The beds take up almost the entire space available. We sleep right through the night and late into the next morning. The hours spent in profound slumber represent so much gained from the war.

Saturday, 19th December.

Yesterday we were right in feeling anxious about our friends. From daybreak onwards the farm has been bombarded over our heads. The shells roar with varying intensity as they pass, according to their size. The little ten-year-old girl, skipping about the yard in her *sabots*, hums out—

"There! That's a 210 at least, and this one a 105. Oh, that little one's but a 77!"

A loud crash, however, sends her flying into the cellar. When she comes up again she tremblingly clutches her mother's skirt. Madame Achain gives her a good shaking.

"What's the matter with you, little stupid?"

"Oh, I'm frightened of the shells!"

"A fine tale, indeed! Look at these *messieurs*, are they frightened?"

These *messieurs*, quietly seated, affect an impassive attitude, to reassure the child.

About three o'clock a lull. We walk over to visit the hospital attendants. A hearty welcome, cups of tea, every one very polite. A couple of armchairs are provided for us by the fireplace. We are treated like lords of a manor.

The Germans are now firing upon Vénizel, some distance farther away. The petrol works seem to be in flames. Our hosts invite us to view the spectacle from the second floor. It is hazy, however, and nothing can be distinguished except a dense cloud of yellowish smoke on the other bank of the Aisne.

"Really, you have no luck at all!" exclaim the attendants; "generally we can make out Vénizel as distinctly as though we were in the town itself."

Soissons also is being violently bombarded.

At night our friends return from the Montagne farm. Varlet affirms—

"We were awfully sorry for you. You missed the *marmites* falling all about your ears."

A couple of projectiles, it seems, had fallen right on to the cattle-shed; a shrapnel had crashed through the dormer-window of the stable where the squadron lay stretched on the ground, and riddled the door with bullets. The section had to take refuge in the grotto-like sheep-fold in the midst of the sheep, now bleating louder than ever.

Sunday, 20th December.

The hours pass very slowly. This morning, for a couple of hours, we had to return to the trenches, to clear away the earth and make them deeper, and so counteract the ravages of the rain.

Back in Bucy, each of us settles down in a corner with a book or newspaper. During the past few days we have resumed a liking for printed characters. People may send us books, no matter on what subject, if only they will help to pass the time. Whatever takes the poor soldier out of a purely animal life to some extent is welcome.

Another shower of projectiles on Bucy. The windows shake and the little girl begins to cry. Madame Achain sighs.

"Do the savages want to demolish our house?"

Suddenly there is a lull. Why does a bombardment begin? Why does it stop? A mystery: the designs of gunners are inscrutable.

Girard, a hospital attendant, pays us a return visit. We thank him for his kind intentions.

"Oh, it's nothing at all," he says.

Is Bucy to become a society rendez-vous? Girard, who just misses falling as he seats himself on a tottering chair, remarks cheerfully—

"What nice quarters you have here!"

Madame Achain is flattered; so are we.

The village streets are strewn with sulphur from to-day's shells. A hayrick has been set on fire and a horse killed close to Madame Maillard's.

Varlet takes me to see this Madame Maillard. Arm in arm we pass along the main street. Right and left ruined and disembowelled houses alternate with buildings almost or wholly intact.

Poor village! Last September it was a pretty little market-town, like many another on the banks of the Aisne, where the houses have a style distinctively their own. The white stone doorways and flights of steps, the violet slate roofs of Champagne and the Ile-de-France, match the staircase gables of neighbouring Flanders. Now the bright, cheerful houses are dilapidated and shattered; the tax-collector's house is empty, so is the baker's. Nor has the church been spared; the recent cannonade has added to the former ruin and desolation.

The civilians, too, are away. We talk to those who have stayed, and daily make progress in the dialect of the place. We know that *ce ch'tiot ila* means "this little boy," as we have already discovered that parents and grandparents call themselves *tayons* and *ratayons*. Brave civilians! No one ever mentions them. Now, this isn't right. Not only have they seen the young ones leave for the front, not only do they live through the horrors of war, but many of them have relations in neighbouring villages occupied by the enemy. Scarcely any are left except women and old men. The latter have passed through 1870; they give their reasons for their present confidence in the result of the war and tell of the miseries of former days.

On the town hall square are drawn up the carriages of the regimental train. Opposite are two ruined hovels and a farm, the roof of which has fallen in, a yard strewn with debris, now the playground of dogs and cats, ducks and hens. Between two calcined pieces of wall stands Madame Maillard's little house. We knock at the door.

"Come in!"

We now find ourselves in one of the gayest corners of Bucy; a very select place, moreover, to which one can only gain admittance by introduction. Here Milliard the postman is the oracle, along with Henriot, his acolyte. Here lodges the *train de combat*, i.e. the conductors of the regimental carriages. These infantry, who ride on horseback all the same, form a separate corporation. Even their dress is different from that of other soldiers: leather jackets and spurs. Their names are Charlot, Petit-Louis, and Grand-Victor. Their functions take them to Soissons and bring them daily into contact with the rearguard service.

Varlet, as a friend, has requested permission to introduce me. His request has been backed by Milliard and Henriot.

"Bring him along, then," they said.

At any hour of the day one can always find at Madame Maillard's white wine, cards and tobacco. In a corner Henriot is sorting the letters. Milliard, after noting the parcels in a book, encloses them in a big bag.

"Are the letters for Achains' ready?" asks Varlet.

"Yes, here's the packet. We will bring you the parcels shortly."

The first thing we do on our return is to shout out—

"We have each had a pint of white wine at the *train de combat*."

"White wine, impossible! You lucky fellows!"

I have no idea why white wine is so scarce. In war there are hosts of things one cannot understand at all.

Monday, 21st December.

During the night a regiment of territorials have arrived who have not yet seen fire. They make a fine *début*, for Bucy is subjected to a heavier bombardment than ever; explosions for three hours without a break. A rain of iron splinters and balls falls upon the roof of our lodging. The tiles come toppling down into the yard. Varlet, who has gone for some of the famous white wine to the *train de combat*, rushes into the room, looking horribly scared as he clasps three bottles to his breast. At the corner of the street he had encountered two shrapnels.

"The first," he said, "went on its way, but I thought the second had got me. It knocked a piece off the doorpost beneath which I had rushed for shelter."

"Oh, *you* wouldn't have been any great loss, but the bottles— —"

The house shakes with the shock of the explosions, which come nearer and nearer. *Sabots* are clattering in the yard. The Achains and the women from neighbouring houses hurry to take refuge in the cellar. We should be wise to follow their example. That, however, would mean leaving the lunch, which is simmering on the fire! Besides, there's something attractive in the idea of brazening the thing out.

The explosions continue. By way of the chimney, which serves as an acoustic tube, we hear the dull, distant detonation as the shell leaves the gun, then the hissing sound, which increases in volume, and finally the violent explosion a few yards away.

A projectile crashes through the roof of the house opposite.

"Suppose we go and see how they are getting along in the cellar?" anxiously suggests Jules.

In a corner crouch the Achains and five or six other women. Sighs and lamentations; invocations to Jesus and Mary!

"Is the house demolished?" asks Madame Achain.

"No, not yet."

At this very moment a shell bursts in the yard.

Ten minutes afterwards, Maxence, who prefers to be more at his ease, mutters—

"It's not very pleasant here. I'm going up."

We follow him. The six of us return to the common room above. Well, suppose we lunch. We take our places at the table, whilst Jacquard carries a pan full of haricot beans to the refugees in the cellar.

Finally the bombardment ceases. Once more the streets are strewn with sulphur. By a miracle nothing is set on fire. A light infantryman and eight horses are killed. Some more rubbish is scattered about the village, where, by the way, life is soon going on as usual.

At five the company returns to the front line. The engineers have constructed shelters for the squadron, six feet below the surface, stoutly propped up by large pieces of timber. One of these tiny habitations is assigned to us, a tolerably warm and perfectly secure sort of room, where one can come for a nap between two watches, and, a more important matter, speak aloud, smoke, and light candles. The shelters of the previous days, being unsupported, have all been washed away by the rain.

Then comes a violent fusillade, beginning far away to the left, with a sound as of rending cloth; it spreads over the whole line. The lieutenant comes out of his dug-out; he orders Jacquard and myself to start the beacon burning.

We both try to light the great acetylene lantern, opening the tap when it should be closed, and closing it when it should be open. At last, to our great surprise, the flame bursts forth. A corporal leaps on the little fuse-projecting rifle and fires it. The fuses rise into the air and fall to the ground, shedding a strong white light over a radius of three hundred yards.

Sergeant Chaboy gives the command to fire. So we load and fire, until our rifles are burning hot. Each man's hundred and fifty cartridges are all gone in less than an hour. Firing slackens on both sides. A sudden return to a state of dead calm.

Munitions are distributed around. Only one man wounded in the 24th: a corporal, who was with a patrol that went out just before the alarm. He was surprised by the fusillade when on the point of rejoining his men, who had already returned to the trench. Caught between two fires, he crouched behind a small elevation, and instinctively protected his head with his right arm. This arm received six bullets,

French and German alike. The sergeant in command of the patrol goes out into the hail of iron to bring back the wounded man, and returns intact, though his clothes are torn to shreds and his hands are all blood-stained. The corporal's arm is reduced to pulp, and his thigh has also received a ball. The hæmorrhage is stopped as well as circumstances permit.

The lieutenant comes round and says—

"Keep your eyes open, the attack will certainly recommence."

Has there really been an attack?

"They do that sort of thing to prevent our falling asleep," growls one man.

The rain has stopped. Each man leans against the trench wall and groups form. We converse in low tones, hiding the light of the pipes in the hollow of the hand, and await events.

At midnight a fresh alarm. The fusillade upon Crouy begins again, and in a few seconds is raging along the entire line. The cannon also are firing. The field of beetroots is lit up by fuses. We maintain an uninterrupted fire under the quiet command of Sergeant Chaboy. A few balls ricochet into the trenches and eight men are wounded.

After forty-five minutes of furious firing everything again becomes calm. A few more salvos and a final crackling of the *mitrailleuses*, and it is over. Profound silence throughout the rest of the night. We cannot understand it.

The company has spent thirty thousand cartridges, perhaps without killing a single German.

Tuesday, 22nd December.

Still in the first line, though in a sector farther away from the enemy.

Reymond invites a few friends to inaugurate an exhibition of drawings he has just finished. Into the recesses of the trench walls enormous beetroots are fitted. On the slices of these hard white roots (they resemble in no way the beetroot of the salad-bowl), cut clean through with a chop from a spade, Reymond has sketched, with a violet crayon, some of the heads of the section.

Here, with its prominent skull and nose, we have the pessimist Mauventre, who at the faintest distant roar of the cannon sighs—

"Here come the *marmites*! They'll be the death of us all yet, see if they're not!"

Reymond has well caught the anxious, troubled features of this intrepid soldier.

On another slice of beetroot is the droll silhouette of Corporal Davor, his startled face almost hidden between his shoulders and his arms akimbo. Davor goes about, at night-time, to stir up those on sentry duty.

"Keep a watch on the right. Keep a watch on the left."

One source of diversion for us is to assume, whenever he passes, the indifferent air of one who ridicules the German attacks.

We all figure in the collection. Varlet is a striking type, with his badger profile immoderately lengthened out by a pipe in the form of a shell or conch, which appears to be soldered on to his nose.

The beetroot haunts our very dreams. Since we are fated to be tormented with the beetroot for all eternity, we may as well extract what fun we can from it.

CHAPTER XI

CHRISTMAS

Wednesday, 23rd December.

The third day in the front line. The section is on guard at the telephone. There is a good *gourbi* or hut provided for each half-section. Two hours' sentry duty on the Vregny road, along which a spent ball comes whistling from time to time.

A pleasant diversion; Captain P—— of the Flying Corps arrives from Paris in a motor-car, and sends for Reymond and myself.

We go down to the car, which has come to a halt below the grotto. Muddy and slimy, enveloped in multi-coloured wrappings, rifle and cartridges hanging on to our persons, pipes in mouth and bearded faces, dirty and grimy, we all the same greet the captain with a very martial military salute.

He has brought us an enormous hamper of provisions. What luck! We are now assured of keeping up Christmas-eve. He also brings us letters, and offers to take back any messages from ourselves. In a dreamy maze of wonder we gaze upon this astonishing individual, who will be in Paris to-night, and whose surroundings are something else than fields of beetroots.

Whilst engaged in conversation, a 150 shell falls a few yards from the car. It fails to explode.

Captain P—— briefly gives us the news. The war will last longer than people think; perhaps another five or six months. We ourselves, it appears, are in a very quiet sector, neither attacked nor attacking, just mounting guard.

Thursday, 24th December.

A bright sun, fine and cold weather. The company go down to the grotto, where they are to sleep to-night. Consequently we shall celebrate our Christmas-eve "beneath these vaults of stone" as the song goes in *Don Carlos*.

Here comes the postman. What a heap of parcels! We spend the afternoon in unpacking them; the war is forgotten; our main preoccupation is to prepare a dinner to which the squadron will all contribute. Jules has gone down to Bucy; for once he has received the lieutenant's permission. His errand is to bring back some wine.

Crouching in a corner, with a bayonet-candlestick by my side, I write away. The man next to me becomes irritated by my silence and evident preoccupation.

"What are you writing?" he asks.

"A letter to my servant."

"Well! That's the very last thing I should have expected you to do."

"You fool! I'm giving her instructions to send out my New Year's gifts, telling her to buy boxes of sweets and chocolates, and giving her the addresses to which they are to be sent, with my card."

No sooner have I spoken than a whole string of epithets—snob, *poseur*, dandy—comes down on my devoted head. I reply in very dignified fashion—

"Oh, indeed! Then you cannot even tolerate ordinary politeness in a man?"

"Politeness! Just look at yourself in a mirror. You would be better employed in giving yourself a scrub down."

At eight o'clock the corner of the grotto containing the first squadron is illuminated with a goodly number of candles.

In the first place, for a successful Christmas-eve celebration we must have some sourcrout—Alsatian, of course. There are five large tins of it, along with a knuckle of ham. Then follow all kinds of sausages, one of which has come from Milan. We speedily dispatch it, at the same time exhorting our "Latin sister" to join in with us. Carried away by an irresistible impulse, the squadron takes by assault several *pâtés de foie gras*. The dessert is most varied: pears, oranges, preserves in jars, in tubes and in pails, a pudding which flames up when you apply a match to it, and, last of all, a drink which the cook has most carefully prepared: coffee with the real odour of coffee.

It is past ten o'clock. The bottles are empty. Every one is very gay and lively; no one intoxicated.

So pleasant an evening cannot end without music.

The concert begins with our old marching songs, those we used to sing at drill, or when tramping the dusty roads, to quicken our speed, songs which we run the risk of forgetting in this accursed war where we scarcely stir a foot. The words are not invariably to be recommended, but the familiar swing and rhythm which used to make us forget the weight of our haversacks, this evening make us forget our burdens of worry and *ennui*. Most conscientiously do we brawl out the tunes. The great advantage of the grotto lies in the fact that one can shout as loud as one pleases.

The lieutenant lifts up the tent canvas with which we have barricaded our den.

"Well! This is something like! You are doing it! May I come in?"

"Of course, *mon lieutenant!*"

We give him a seat on an empty bag, and the concert recommences.

Singers, with some pretence to a voice, try hard to carry off their sentimental or grandiloquent ditties, but it is the motley repertoire of absurdity and ridicule that meets with the success of the evening: the songs of Montmartre, artistes' refrains, fertile in spicy nonsense. We mark time by tapping our empty plates with the back of the hand. The noisy merriment is intensified when we come to the chorus.

With frenzied enthusiasm the squadron shouts out the chorus of Hervé's *Turcs*—

> *Nous, nous sommes les soldats*
> *Et nous marchons au pas,*
> *Plus souvent au trépas....*

And now Charensac comes forward.

"Make way for the Ambassador of Auvergne," barks out Varlet.

"Quite right, I am from Auvergne, and I'm going to dance the *bourrée*."

He dances it, all alone. Some of the audience, making a humming sound with their hands, the rest whistling or else beating time with cans and *gamelles*, form an improvised orchestra, half Spanish, half negro. The dancer's big round face, flanked with little tufts of black whiskers, lights up. He is both the Auvergnat and his betrothed—advancing, receding, seeming to escape from himself. When you think he is utterly exhausted, he still finds it possible to shout out in joyous accents—

"Now, ladies and gentlemen, a collection for 'l'artisse.'"

And he mimics in succession a lion-tamer and a lady walking the tight rope. The sous rain down into his *képi*.

Thereupon Charensac strikes a lyrical vein. He sings in the *patois* of Auvergne, and, being in an expansive mood, relates the whole of his life, from his birth down to the present day, forgetting nothing, not even his wedding festivities, in the course of which he assures us that he thrashed his mother-in-law.

Charensac's eloquence is made up of hiccoughs and invocations, songs and laughter, but we understand all the same. We gather that this giant of an Auvergnat is a compound of landowner, estate manager, Government official, and representative of his syndicate at the *Bourse du Travail*. I find I have had to come to the front to learn that a keen sense of the rights of property is not incompatible with the spirit of revolutionary claims.

Charensac stops for a moment, exhausted. Thereupon Reymond, who has had his eyes fixed on him for some time, leans on his elbow, and from the corner in which he has been lying, remarks—

"You don't know whom you make me think of, Charensac, always shouting and stuffing like a huge ogre? I'll tell you; you remind me of old Ubu."

"Who's old Ubu?" asks the other.

"Old Ubu——" begins Reymond.

Startled, I burst out—

"You're not going to tell the first squadron who old Ubu was?"

"Don't you interrupt."

And Reymond explains. In profound silence we listen as he relates how Ubu was the first man who recommended that eight bullets should be put into a rifle, because with eight bullets it is possible to kill eight of the enemy, and you have that number the less to account for. The thing that delights the first squadron is Ubu's prophetic description of the modern battle: "... We have the foot-soldiers at the foot of the hill ... the cavalry behind them to burst upon the jumbled mass of combatants, and the artillery round by the windmill here to fire upon them all." The men clap their hands in delight and exclaim knowingly: "Yes, that's it! The very thing!"

Finally Reymond says that Ubu, like Charensac, was a sort of enormous giant, with a voice of thunder and an insatiable appetite.

After this, Charensac is never called anything but old Ubu, and as the sly rascal sees here a new excuse for the satisfaction of his appetites, he accepts the surname with enthusiasm.

Old Ubu will become popular in the 352nd Regiment, and rightly so. In warfare it is necessary to evoke the shade of Jarry as frequently as that of Homer.

Midnight. A procession of magi moves along the galleries. Reymond, a muffler wrapped turban-wise round his head and majestically draped in the folds of a poncho, carries the myrrh in a *gamelle*. The tent pickets serve the purpose of sceptres. Some one walks backwards in front of the kings, with an electric lamp raised above his head. This represents the star.

The star guides us back to our *crèche*, where the candles have just flickered out. Kings and shepherds lie *pêle-mêle* on the ground, and the loud snoring soon proves them to be sound asleep.

Friday, 25th December.

At half-past six the sergeants shout into the grotto—

"Up, 24th, and fully equipped!"

"What's this?... What's the matter?"

"Get up at once; within a quarter of an hour we must be in the fighting line."

Each man, half-awake, puts on his boots and his puttees and fastens on his haversack.

Muster in front of the grotto: a frightful din. From Crouy to Vailly every single battery keeps up an uninterrupted fire on the German trenches. What an awakening we are giving them for their Christmas!

In a few words the lieutenant explains the day's programme—

"Attacks on the left as soon as the bombardment is over. In front of Bucy we are commanded not to move. The 24th must hold the support trenches and keep in readiness 'for any eventuality.'"

The usual thing!

This morning the fighting emplacements are not very dangerous. The company deploys along the path which skirts the ridge on a level with the grotto. This is the first line as it was at the beginning of November; to-day the first line is over five hundred yards forward.

Men belonging to the 23rd relate how the Germans have been singing hymns all night long. They must have been celebrating their triumphs; our artillery will bring them all back to their senses. The shells hammer away at the frozen soil, tearing it up when they explode. Impossible to hear oneself speak in the midst of the uproar. The sky is pale blue, gradually assuming a darker tint. The sun is shining brightly, but it affords no warmth. Each man sends out from his mouth tiny clouds with every breath.

On the road between the loop-holes there are still to be seen some of the branch-constructed shelters in which we lodged a couple of months ago. With the exception of two on sentry duty, we are going to finish here our interrupted Christmas dreams.

In war-time, unless he is sent on guard or given fatigue duty, the foot-soldier makes his bed anywhere and anyhow. In case he has insufficient room he shrinks into as small space as possible, his knees touching his chin. The cartridge cases of the man behind him dig into his ribs, and those of the man in front crush his stomach, the hilt of the bayonet finds a place between two other ribs, whilst the sheath always seems twisted and bent.... Well, it can't be helped. You just settle down as well as you can, and you dream, whether awake or asleep.

From time to time some one will growl out, "Its impossible to sleep with such a noise going on!" and off he falls at once into a deep slumber.

A joyless day seems in store for us. Shall we be attacked? Or are we to attack?

A brief distraction takes the form of a young mouse, which comes out of its hole close to our feet, and is by no means startled by the sight of six *poilus* seated around on the floor. Soon it scampers away, but immediately reappears and fastens its impudent eyes upon us. The roar of the cannon does not seem to disturb its tiny ears. It is neutral. I quietly put out my hand, but evidently the gesture is too familiar, for the mouse re-enters its trench and appears no more.

At two o'clock the 24th are ordered to equip and muster. It appears that we are to relieve the 23rd in the first line.

News arrives: our attack in the direction of Crouy has succeeded only partially. The artillery duel is coming to an end. We appreciate the silence that follows.

We are fixed up in the first line. I spend a couple of hours with Verrier at the listening post, anything but a pleasant spot. The Germans are fifty yards away. By risking an eye at the loop-hole we distinctly make out their wires and the mounds of earth behind which they are. At night we have to keep our ears alive to the faintest sound to prevent ourselves from being taken prisoners or massacred by a patrol party.

An interlude. The Germans are imitating the cries of various animals: cock and dog, calf and pig.

We ask for news of the Kaiser. They reply—

"He's quite well, thanks. We'll see you again shortly in Paris."

A single though expressive word is our retort.

Again they shout to us from the enemy's trenches—

"A merry Christmas! Send us some wine."

Then they sing the *Marseillaise*!

Saturday, 26th December.

This morning we found the water frozen in our cans.

The cooks, when bringing in the soup, assure us that the Hindus have been sent for to make an attack on Crouy. They describe minutely how they are dressed.

"There is a fellow in the *train de combat*," says "the Fireman," "who has come across them at Soissons."

Thereupon Jacquard cannot contain himself for joy. Being of a most optimistic temperament, he sees the Sikhs and Gurkhas coming down Hill 132 and cutting our invaders' throats. He endeavours to give his foolish face an expression of ferocity, and explains how the Hindus attack.

"The beggars glide about noiselessly in the dark, like serpents. Impossible to hear them coming. Before you are aware they are upon you, cutting your throat with the big knife they hold between their teeth...."

"*Bigre!* Lucky for us they're on our side."

But where has Jacquard, who has never travelled beyond the neighbourhoods of the Rue de Sentier and Levallois-Perret, obtained such detailed information about the warlike habits of these distant peoples?

Meanwhile there is a dead calm; they forget to relieve us. The section returns to Bucy after forty hours' outpost duty. We quarter in a half-ruined house which contains scarcely enough room to lie down in. We sleep in higgledy-piggledy fashion with our comrades, the feet of one man against the face of another, and vice versa.

Sunday, 27th December.

No means of returning to the Achains', the company being fixed up at the other extremity of the village. I knock at the door of the Ronchards, the brother and sister who showed us hospitality one afternoon last month. They place at our disposal a large well-warmed room, where we can all six sleep on an enormous litter of straw.

Mademoiselle Ronchard has not yet recovered from her disappointment at our not eating her rabbit stew. The stove begins to roar and we come back to life again.

A detail: we find ourselves covered with fleas. An energetic hunt commences. It is not without results.

We hear a voice in the street and rush out. The Montagne farm is a mass of flame, the result of a bombardment which has lasted several hours. The entire hill is illumined; even from this distance we can hear the roar of the fire. Beams fall to the ground and flames of fire rise into the air. Dark silhouettes are seen in the neighbourhood. Without a word we gaze long at the sinister spectacle. Some one simply remarks—

"The pity of it all!"

We return to the Ronchards.

Monday, 28th December.

Thaw and rain, creating mud and all the old troubles over again. We remain indoors at the Ronchards'.

How calm and quiet this evening! There are six of us, feet in slippers, sitting round the table. Some are reading, others writing by the soft light of a lamp. Are we the same persons who, only the day before yesterday, were wallowing in the trench between two walls of mud? Are we really at war, at the front, with the enemy less than a mile away? Our friends and relatives, whose letters betray constant anxiety on our behalf, invariably imagine us in the thick of the fight. If only they could know, this very moment, that we are in such comfortable quarters, that there is such an element of peace in our sad surroundings!

The howling wind makes us appreciate by contrast the joy of being under cover. The distant firing sounds like the noise made by a cart as it jolts along over the pavings.

Tuesday, 29th December.

An hour's drill this morning in the shell-ploughed fields, manual exercise and section school, just to remind us that we are soldiers. Hair review by the lieutenant in the afternoon. The entire company must pass through the barber's hands.

Charensac bursts into our room, shouting out, "Good day. How are you, my young friends?" His voice upsets us completely, and we roughly inquire whether he has not yet learnt the value of silence after five months of warfare. Thereupon he explains in his gibberish—

"Don't get angry. I know some one at Crouy who has received a supply of benedictine and all sorts of good things to eat. I at once thought of you, for I know my generous little mates will pay for me a drink...."

He is absolved. A bottle of benedictine is worth considering at certain moments of one's life, and so Charensac starts for Crouy, supplied with funds, precise instructions, and promises.

In ordinary times the road to Crouy is probably as good as any other road. But these are not ordinary times. Shells are continually falling, and a portion of the village of Crouy itself is in the hands of the enemy. A German machine-gunner, whom we know well, opens fire when any one passes a certain corner. Charensac, however, disdains the very idea of peril; he is very brave. The other day, when he was brawling away as usual, his weary neighbour interrupted him—

"*Ah! là, là,* you wouldn't make such a noise if we were attacking."

Charensac replied, not without an air of dignity, speaking instinctively of himself in the third person, as though he might have been Cæsar or Napoleon—

"Don't trouble yourself about Charensac. Just keep by his side when there is hot work to be done, then no one will ever be in a position to say that you were afraid."

And, as a matter of fact, Charensac continues to make fine sport of war, even in the midst of danger. Certainly I have never met his like before.

Charensac returns in the course of the evening. We all run to meet him. He tosses off a glass of benedictine, accepts a flannel girdle, two pocket-handkerchiefs, a bar of chocolate, a camphor sachet for killing fleas, and then he retires to sleep, shrieking joyfully.

Wednesday, 30th December.

From noon to four o'clock we clean out the branch trenches, which the rain has transformed into mud puddles.

Thursday, 31st December.

Morning drill during a brief spell of sunshine.

Belin comes to dinner.

The year about to begin will be a year of peace and victory, of our return home.

We do not wait for midnight before going to bed, though we first wish one another a happy 1915.

Friday, 1st January, 1915.

Not everybody has followed our example of sobriety in letting in the new year. This morning some unsteady walking is visible in the streets of Bucy and Bacchic songs fill the air.

At five the company returns to the grotto.

Saturday, 2nd January.

A fight against mud, which we scrape away from the road. At noon we proceed to the first line; for some time past, relieving forces have been sent out in the daytime. Passing through the branch is a difficult matter, for we wade in mud up to the knee.

Two hours' duty at the listening post. A calm night. Occasional firing.

Sunday, 3rd January.

The cooks bring in the soup at ten o'clock and inform us that we shall be relieved in the evening instead of at noon. Mud and war! Five more hours of this sort of work! This is what we call, like all good Pickwickians, "Adding insult to injury, as the parrot said when being taught to learn English after being taken from his native land."

From four to six, Verrier and I, facing each other as we lean against the trench walls, await the relief without speaking a word, our eyes obstinately fixed on our boots.

The return at night along the branches; the mud is thicker and more plentiful than ever. Frightful oaths and the continual exhortation—

"Gently ahead! We cannot follow you."

Shades glide behind one another, accompanied by the sound of the *gamelle* chains. The head of the company has already reached the grotto whilst the rear is still waiting in the first line till its turn comes to march away.

The branch opens out on to a very uneven path, scarcely visible through the wood. In the profound darkness we hear the outbursts of rage and the curses of the men. The rifles knock against the branches. There is another path skirting the wood, over exposed ground. A few balls whistle past, chiefly during reliefs. We have to advance in Indian file, carefully planting our feet in the steps of the man in front because of the many holes in the ground. Fifty yards of a steep ascent, slippery as soap. The falls multiply. Wonderful to relate, there are no broken bones; not even a sprained ankle.

At last we reach the grotto. Candles and pipes are lit. Each man removes his equipment and his coat and flings himself on to the straw. After a brief rest we dine, seated round a newspaper which serves for a tablecloth. Our comrades left behind in the grotto have kept the parcels which have arrived whilst we have been in the first line. We manifest a schoolboy's delight in unfastening them.

Monday, 4th January.

In front of the grotto the sections muster in columns of fours. A few stragglers arrive, buckling on their haversacks.

The sergeant welcomes them with the words—

"Don't hurry, I beg of you. I suppose I'm here to wait for you."

The company goes down to Bucy. Within a short time the six of us are installed with the Ronchards.

Another hunt for fleas. A vigorous offensive is necessary to prevent ourselves being devoured alive. The labour required to keep one's body clean becomes something herculean. The mud on coats and puttees refuses to dry. We give up the struggle.

Tuesday, 5th January.

Whilst the rest are away at drill I stay behind, the major having exempted me from duty. I seize the opportunity to do the house work and Jules gives me a helping hand.

It is Jules' dream to become a *valet de chambre* in Paris. His views on life as lived in the capital are unusual and lacking in precision.

He says to me—

"When peace is proclaimed, won't you take me back with you?"

"Listen to me, Jules, I don't want to hurt you, but I cannot afford more than one servant."

"Nonsense, a man like you!"

"Yes, you see how badly society is built up."

Jules goes over his good points—

"You know me well; I can easily adapt myself to things. With me, you may have your mind at peace, I would take charge of everything, and you would not even need to pay me."

Such disinterestedness sends a shudder through me.

"You agree?" asks Jules.

"But—don't you see, I'm tied down here."

"How stupid you are! Things will not always remain as they are now."

"And what if I am killed?"

"Don't talk like that. It would be a pity!"

He sticks to his idea, for he has chosen me to assist him in the realization of his dreams. Finally he remarks—

"You will leave me free to go out whenever I want, won't you? And every morning I'll go and kill some little birds for you."

In the evening we chat away with quite civilian freedom of mind. We forget both what we are engaged upon, and where we are. Plans for the future are discussed without any one thinking of making the remark that our talk is very silly. We pay attention neither to our odd-looking accoutrements, nor to our unshaven chins. We are not even aware of our tired condition.

We go out into the yard for a quiet smoke. It is very mild; the sky is lit up with stars, as in times of peace. Away towards the north we hear the firing of the sentries. The cannon is booming on our left.

Reymond does not feel sleepy; neither do I.

"Suppose we write an article for the *Figaro*?"

Agreed. I set to work. After scribbling away for an hour, I hand a few sheets across to Reymond. After reading them, he declares—

"How idiotic!"

I feel hurt.

"Then write the article yourself, since you are so clever."

"It's not my business; I'm a painter. Begin it all over again."

I obey. More sheets and a further reading by Reymond.

"This time it's not quite so bad. Suppose we go over it word for word."

At two in the morning we are still at it. Our aim is to set forth nothing but facts, and at the same time to thrill our readers.

Wednesday, 6th January.

It's all very well to play at being journalists, and to spend the night in writing, but this morning we must all be ready for drill at half-past seven. The two collaborators are snoring away. Varlet wakes us by walking over our bodies.

"Come now, up! you two journalists."

The journalists refuse to budge.

"You'll be marked absent!"

"Don't trouble about that."

At ten o'clock our comrades return. Our absence has passed unnoticed, the very thing upon which our modesty and laziness combined were relying.

At noon—

"Quick! Muster in half an hour. We return to the trenches."

The usual stir and commotion in alarms of this kind.

Afternoon and night are spent very quietly in the grotto.

Thursday, 7th January.

The 24th occupies fresh positions between Bucy and Crouy, still in the first line. The weather is dreadful; it is useless to gaze through the loop-hole, you cannot see a yard in front of you.

A dull, unpleasant day. This evening, seated by Reymond's side in a dug-out, which luckily is waterproof, I recopy by candle-light the article for the *Figaro,* taking down the words at his dictation, with tongue protruding, like a schoolboy, to make my handwriting more legible. From time to time the rain, oozing through the ceiling, drops a tear-stain on to the copy.

When the sheets of paper are filled, I carefully put them away safe from the wet. They will be in the postman's hands to-morrow.

Four hours' sentry duty now to divert our minds. Those who pass by tell us that the shelters are falling in upon the sleepers. Several times during the night we have to go to the help of our buried comrades.

CHAPTER XII

THE CROUY AFFAIR

Friday, 8th January.

This morning at half-past six, our artillery opens fire over a sector of several kilometres. Fifty guns each fire a hundred and twenty-five shots, a formidable total. The Moroccans carry two lines of trenches above Crouy and, along with the light infantry, obtain a footing on the upland. An important success, it appears. The German counter-attack is ineffectual. Their artillery is directed upon our trenches and upon the ground in the rear.

Are we to attack shortly? The question is asked of the lieutenants, but they cannot answer it.

From noon onwards firing grows more intense; it is a tempest of iron until five o'clock. Storms of German shells beat down upon Bucy, whilst our own 75's crash their projectiles on to the trenches opposite. In the midst of the din we distinctly note the roar of the heavier shells passing overhead with the sound as of a slowly moving train over an iron bridge.

As though the rain were not enough, a hailstorm begins to lash our faces. Thunder-claps alternate with the roar of cannon. The sky is lit up with lightning flashes. We are in a state of utter stupefaction when the hour of relief arrives.

On reaching our Ali-Baba cave, we learn that a 210 shell fell this afternoon in front of the grotto on a spot which for months we have regarded as absolutely sheltered. Sergeant Martin has been hurled into the air and the cooks flung *pêle-mêle* on to the ground. Even in the galleries the men have been lifted off their feet by an irresistible shock. It is discovered that no one has received any real harm except Sergeant Martin, whose left leg has been cut off close to the pelvis. Debris of red cloth and of flesh are still strewn around the enormous hollow dug by the projectile.

Saturday, 9th January.

After a delightful and dry night spent in the grotto, we are sent to clean out the branch trenches. Jacquard remains in the grotto busily occupied in arranging in a box our store of chocolate tablets.

Outside, the dance continues: 75's, 77's, 90's, 105's, 155's, and 210's plough their way through the air. With hands crossed on the shovel handle, and one foot on the iron, we watch these latter shells fall around the Montagne farm, and upon

Le Moncel and Sainte-Marguerite: first a black cloud, then a red star-like flash and finally a thunderous explosion.

The enemy is trying to find our batteries. From time to time four shots from a 75 follow one another in rapid succession as though to say: "Don't concern yourself." The spectacle is so fascinating that we do not feel at all inclined to work.

Violent fusillade from the direction of Crouy.

Towards evening the rain stops a little; so does the firing. The company is again installed in the first line.

Verrier, Reymond, Maxence and myself are appointed to occupy in turn two loop-holes and a dug-out. This latter is not an attractive place: a cavity of three cubic yards dug in the side of the trench. There is scarcely room to move one's body, and a few inside repairs are quite indispensable.

No sooner have we arrived than the corporal in charge declares—

"There are four of you for this post. Arrange amongst yourselves as regards the hours, but I want always to see two of you at the loop-holes."

"All right."

Two of us then mount guard; a simple matter in the daytime. It consists in walking about the trench, smoking one's pipe. An occasional glance opposite to see that nothing stirs.

Those left in the dug-out are busily occupied. First, there is the cleaning to be done. Our predecessors have left bones and pieces of waste paper lying about, and the sight is sickening.

"*Ah, là là!* Could they not have removed their own filth themselves?"

Then three tent canvases are opened out upon one another in front of the entrance to the dug-out. This is a delicate operation: no space or chink must be left between this improvised doorway and the walls of earth; first, in order to stop the draughts—it is extraordinary how one fears draughts in the trenches!—and then to keep out any light calculated to make our presence known to the Germans.

A cover on the ground to serve as a carpet. Two small niches in the wall for placing candles. A piece of plank, held up by two tent pickets driven into the wall, forms a shelf: the refuge of pipes, *gamelles*, and stores. Two bags on the ground to lean upon.

This task ended, one can take breath. It is now the time for letter-writing, the ever-recurring formula: "I am writing to you from the first line of trenches, close to the Germans. All the same, don't be anxious about me, there is little risk...." We read the paper and find that all foot-soldiers are looked upon as heroes. There it is, in print. These things flatter us greatly. After all, it's something to be a foot-soldier!

Generally everything is quiet at this hour; like ourselves, the Germans are preparing dinner and bed.

The time comes for us to sit down to our meal. One man only remains on guard. The other three dine gaily, and at considerable length. When the conversation becomes too noisy, the sentry gives a kick at the tent canvas. Every ten minutes the poor fellow draws aside the screen and asks—

"Aren't you going to relieve me soon? I'm terribly hungry."

We reply—

"All right, there'll be something left for you. Remove that head of yours; you're letting in the cold."

He resigns himself to his lot, well aware that any one under cover is privileged to swear at a wet dog.

From time to time he fires a shot into the dark, just to make him forget his hunger. He puts himself *en liaison* with the entries right and left of him.

Finally he hears the words—

"Come along, your turn for dinner. One of us will take your place. Just wipe your boots and don't soil the carpet."

He glides into the hole, which exhales a blended odour of stew, tobacco and fighting. A broad smile appears on his face as he says: "That smells nice." And he believes it too. He perceives his portion simmering away on a soldier's chafing-dish. Speedily comes fresh cause for anxiety—

"Where's my coffee? I'll wager you've not kept it warm for me!"

Indignant protests.

"See! There's your coffee. We've even kept a cigar for you. Would you like to begin with a couple of sardines?"

After which, his hosts add, pretending to shiver with cold—

"Careful, all the same, you're wet through. Don't stir, or you'll upset everything in the room."

At eight o'clock' dinner is over. Each man cleans his plate and his knife and fork with a piece of bread.

Preparations for the night. Two are going on watch duty and two to sleep; relieving one another every four hours. The two privileged ones, who are able to digest their meal at leisure, light their pipes, pass the bottle of spirits, and are speedily fast asleep.

The two sentries stand with their back's to the rain. They hide their pipes in the hollow of the hand.

"What weather!"

"Dreadful!"

One man coughs. The other remarks—

"Suppose we move from here; you'll wake the children."

Maxence and myself occupy the dug-out from eight till midnight. We smoke a few pipes. The post has brought newspapers. Our accoutrements hang on nails driven into the timber which props up the shelter. Maxence, who has been somewhat fidgety for some minutes, remarks—

"I don't care! I'm going to put on my socks; it will be far more comfortable."

"And suppose the lieutenant comes along.... And what if the Germans attack?"

"Eh?"

He hesitates, his hand on the point of unrolling his puttee.

"Nonsense! Those over in front won't stir an inch."

I succeed in persuading him not to remove his boots. Well wrapped in our coverings, we talk before going to sleep.

I am interrupted by an exclamation in the trench—

"The Germans are in the branch trench! Look out!"

We spring to our accoutrements and arms. A hundred yards to the right a brisk fusillade is going on.

"Who was it shouted, 'Look out!'?"

"A man of the fourth section, the one on guard at the listening post," placidly answers Verrier, who has already fixed his bayonet to his rifle, though retaining his cigarette between his lips.

"Well! Where are the Germans? There is nothing to be heard!"

We begin to scent one of those tragi-comic incidents frequent in warfare. The lieutenant passes, an electric lamp in hand. As he strides away towards the right, he gives the order—

"Everybody at the loop-holes!"

The command is obeyed.

In half an hour's time he returns.

"Well! What was the matter?"

Thereupon, half-smiling, and half-angry, he relates—

"It was a German patrol that had taken the wrong direction. Our sentry was watching, sheltered by a tarpaulin stretched across two pieces of wood. He hears the sound of voices and heavy steps, and, crash! something splits the tarpaulin and falls with a howl on to his shoulders. It was a German! Stupefied, the sentry calls out: 'To arms!' Everybody comes rushing from the shelters, and there is a fine uproar. Meanwhile, the German scales the parapet and clears off. The patrol had already disappeared."

When the lieutenant has gone, we make our way through the three or four hundred yards of deserted, winding branches to visit the heroes of the adventure. They look very shamefaced.

The corporal seems uneasy.

"Do you think the lieutenant will give me the lock-up for this?"

Indignantly he adds—

"But what fools they were to come along here! Is that the way an enemy patrol goes to work?"

Evidently, if the enemy in future approaches our lines without taking the usual precautions, he will no longer be playing the game!

The sentry especially has a very sickly look.

"Why didn't you stick your bayonet into the fool of a German?" some one asks.

"My bayonet was sheathed. Do you fix your bayonet when on sentry duty in the trench? It's only in the illustrated papers that you find such silly things!"

The escaped German, whom we baptize Fritz, has left his Mauser behind. What sort of a story will Fritz have to tell on returning to his own lines without his rifle? Will he be kicked unmercifully? Or will he be clever enough to make up a tale of heroism which will win him an iron cross?

A stormy night. Rifle shots. Patrols peppering one another.

The voice of a wounded German calls for help, a plaintive, wailing voice; he wishes to surrender, his comrades have left him, and he begs us to come for him.

"Come along. We'll do you no harm."

There is no reply. Most likely a feint to draw some of us into an ambush.

Sunday, 10th January.

This morning we notice that the Germans have profited by the darkness to dig an attack branch, enabling them to pour a raking fire into our trenches. This part of the sector is becoming difficult to hold. We receive the impression that the enemy is preparing an ugly surprise.

At noon we are relieved. The glorious sunshine puts us in good humour. A profound sense of security and repose inside—or in front of—the grotto, whilst a heavy cannonade is preparing an attack on Hill 132.

The attack is made at sunset. The Moroccans and light infantry carry a third line of trenches, and fortify themselves on the upland, almost touching the Perrière farm.

Monday, 11th January.

The whole afternoon we stand at the entrance of the grotto watching the big projectiles fall upon Bucy. *Vr—ran! vr—ran!* In the evening, silence again reigns; the 21st and 24th go down to Vénizel, on the Aisne, a distance of four kilometres from Bucy.

For the first time since the 15th of November we are about to find ourselves out of rifle-shot range. How glad we should be if we could put ourselves for a week out of earshot of the cannons' roar!

It rains in torrents. Our quarters have been badly arranged; no one knows where he has to go. Lieutenants shout; sub-officers raise their arms in despair. We men wait, the rain pouring down upon us.

Finally comes an order: our squadron is on guard, and we must occupy a pinnace moored on the right bank of the Aisne, above the bridge. We follow the banks of the swollen stream, and then cross a wood, the first few trees of which are partially under water. A faint light is seen: it is the pinnace. We enter one by one along a shaky plank which threatens to give way. And now we are yachtsmen. This is one of the most curious incarnations of our life as soldiers.

The squadron—which, for the occasion, we call the crew—occupies the 'tween decks. There is a big petrol lamp and a good stove. The skipper, mobilized on the spot, and his wife, seem very nice people. And what a pleasant refuge!

Varlet brings letters and parcels. Our joy knows no bounds. Reymond, tricked out in a sky-blue cap, repeatedly mounts on to the deck.

"Are you on the watch?" asks the corporal.

"Yes. Fine breeze north-north-west. In twenty days we shall reach the Cape of Good Hope."

With a stubby little pipe in his mouth, his shaggy beard, and his manner of walking with legs apart as though the boat were rolling, he looks exactly like a seasoned old salt.

There are fourteen of us in the boat, and we are all covered with vermin. The corporal, neck and breast bare, is engaged in minutely picking his shirt; he burns his fleas in the stove, and at each immolation gives an exclamation of wild satisfaction.

The capotes are hardened with mud, and the bayonets, which usually serve as candlesticks, are covered with wax drippings. As for our rusty, stopped-up rifles, they will only be fit for service after a thorough cleaning.

I feel somewhat feverish, and sit down apart from the rest. A formidable slap on my back: Charensac's way of showing his affection. Heart-broken to see me ill, he shouts confidentially into my ear—

"What's the use of fretting, old fellow?"

"Just leave him alone for the present," advises the corporal.

Charensac brightens up more and more as he eats. He is just as happy and pleased in a pinnace as he would be anywhere else.

Seeing that his comrades are writing letters, he goes to and fro, brawling out—

"Ah! ah! So my little mates are working. Good! Mustn't disturb them now."

In spite of the smell of rancid oil and tar we are quite content because we are dry, and so we sit up till two in the morning. Finally, each of us picks out a corner, wraps himself in his cover, and falls asleep on the floor.

Tuesday, 12th January.

The whole morning on the deck of the pinnace. An infernal cannonade is roaring on the upland. How they must be enjoying themselves! About eleven o'clock, as I was beginning to brush my capote, Charensac and Meuret come running up, out of breath, and sputter out—

"To arms! The Germans are advancing."

Various exclamations. We hastily equip ourselves.

When the section is mustered, the lieutenant first makes us cross the bridge of Vénizel and pass along the left bank of the Aisne, i.e. in the direction opposite to the seat of battle. Here we begin to descend with the stream. The swollen waters, of slimy yellow, carry off debris of every kind. After proceeding a kilometre, we reach a wooden bridge. The flood is so strong that the current threatens to wash over the flooring. This bridge has been constructed by the English; it still bears inscriptions in their language. We cross; again we find ourselves on the right bank. To reach the trenches we shall have to traverse, in open daylight, the plain of Vénizel, which is three kilometres wide, and under the enemy's fire from the neighbouring heights.

"In columns by twos, forward!"

Scarcely have we started in the direction of Bucy than we are greeted by a shell, then by two, followed soon by three. We are being fired upon. A command is given that the four squadrons should follow one another at intervals of fifty yards.

On reaching the first houses in Bucy we find considerable excitement. Gunners, sword and revolver in hand, exclaim—

"Don't go in that direction! The Germans are at the sugar-mill of Crouy."

A horseman gallops up, coming from the line. As he rides past we ask—

"Well, good news?"

He frowns and makes a wry face. Evidently there is hard fighting going on.

The section climbs in the direction of the trenches. Half-way up, we meet a few men and a lieutenant of another regiment. They wear a haggard look, and seem uncertain of their movements.

"Where are you going?" asks our lieutenant.

"I've not the faintest idea," says the other. "This is all that's left of my company. We have just been mined."

One man, still in a very shaky condition, explains—

"For days past we have been hearing a scraping noise underground. Then, of a sudden, *v'lan*! We are all blown into the air! Our poor comrades!"

Over the entire upland, between Missy, Bucy, Crouy, and the Paris-Soissons-Maubeuge road, the battle is being waged. The Germans counter-attack at several points. The artillery duel is a terrible one.

I am quite out of breath. As well as I can, aided by Charensac, I climb the steep and muddy slope leading to the first-line trenches. Really, I must throw out some ballast.

Thrusting my hand into my *musette*, I take out a couple of tins of preserved lobster. These I mechanically hand across to Charensac, who, woebegone, makes a sign that he does not want them. This is one of the saddest impressions of fatigue and weariness that I have ever experienced. If Charensac has come to this pass, we *are* in a state! I say—

"Well, then; the more's the pity! Away they go!"

I fling the two tins on to the road, Charensac sighing as he watches them disappear.

At the top of the slope we start along the hollow way bordering the upland. We are up to our knees in mud. Exhausted, I sit down on the ground, but a shrapnel explosion a few yards away proves to me that this is neither the time nor the place to rest.

I rejoin the section just as it is passing close to a battery installed above the way, and partially concealed by foliage. The captain walks to and fro under the balls. Accosting our lieutenant, he asks—

"Where are you going?"

A vague gesture is the reply.

"You don't know? Then come along with me, you can defend my guns."

We have to pass before one of those mouths spitting out fire without a break. Our lieutenant politely remarks that it might be prudent to interrupt the firing, to avoid accidents. The captain, with a somewhat disdainful smile, condescends to give the order—

"Cease firing, to allow the foot-soldiers to pass."

Our section disappears in a branch in front of the four cannons. Some men keep watch and fit up loop-holes and firing embankments. The rest fling themselves on to the ground. The enemy's artillery plays upon us. A 77 shell, which does not explode, comes to a stop on the edge of the parapet, close to a gabion. Its pointed nose projects over the trench as though to see what is taking place.

Charensac glides up to my side with the two tins of lobster in his hands! On reflecting over the matter, he could not tolerate the loss of such wealth, and so, at the risk of a dose of shrapnel, he actually went back to pick up my preserved food. It's a case of principle; not only will he waste nothing himself, he will not see anything belonging to others wasted. And he actually refuses to accept them for himself! I finally overcome his scruples by reasoning with him somewhat as follows: "I tell you I threw them away, they are not mine. Keep them yourself, you old fool. And take care that the Germans let you live long enough to eat them."

He thanks me heartily for the trouble he has taken.

The day ends without any serious incidents to ourselves. When evening comes, the section retires into a dug-out. A piece of bread and a tin of *foie gras* is all we have to eat after a twenty-four hours' fast. At eleven o'clock comes the order to rejoin the rest of the 24th. The company is put on reserve, and we go to sleep in a neighbouring grotto.

Five in the morning. In obedience to command, I rise, but find that I can scarcely stand on my legs. I am quite sick; on trying to put on my things, a feeling of dizziness comes over me.

I give up the struggle and stagger away to see the lieutenant.

"Mon lieutenant, I feel ill and can scarcely stand."

"Yes, that's very evident."

"Do you think there will be anything of importance happening to-day?"

"I don't think so; the company is now in reserve. Remain here. You may go down to the hospital shortly."

I lie down again in a corner, on a pile of stones, which seems as soft as eider-down, so great is my fatigue. By candle-light my companions rapidly equip and arm themselves. Reymond and Verrier, Maxence and Jacquard, disappear; I have not even the strength to call after them *au revoir!* Henriot and Varlet grasp me by the hand.

"Come now, old fellow, you're not dead yet."

"I feel very near it."

"You'll soon be all right. See you again shortly."

And off they go. I am left alone in this unfamiliar grotto, which is larger, colder, and more forbidding in appearance than our former one. I again fall into a heavy sleep.

Ten o'clock. A succession of dull sounds is heard above the vault: the roar of cannon. I hear whispers and wailings. A relief post has just been installed in the grotto, and I recognize the voices of the major and the attendants. Stretcher-bearers continue to bring in one wounded man after another. What can be the matter?

I sit up. They tell me that fighting has been going on over the whole upland for more than four hours.

"And where is the 24th?"

"The 24th is in reserve."

Good. I lie down again and instantly sink off to sleep.

Noon. The same dull heavy sounds, even more frequent than a couple of hours ago. I rise to my feet, still in a very shaky condition. No one is near me, except a few wounded Moroccans who have dragged themselves here. Somewhat uneasy, I proceed to the entrance of the grotto. The spectacle is a bewildering one. Squalls of shells are falling; bullets are whistling past. About twenty yards away are a few straggling soldiers, firing and shouting. A light infantryman, with glaring eyes, screams out—

"A rifle! Give me a rifle! Mine won't fire any longer. A rifle! Here they come!"

And the wounded drag themselves painfully along, trying to find shelter. I question one of them. Things are going ill with us. The Germans are advancing; they will be here any moment.

A lieutenant, as he passes, calls out—

"Those of you who are wounded and are able to walk, go back, unless you want to be taken prisoners."

Go back. An easy thing to say. I know the ways leading to the hospital, they catch all the spent balls; besides, the German artillery must be sweeping the slopes.

Moreover, I cannot stand upright. Now I'm in for it, I shall surely be taken. A feeling of inexpressible anguish comes over me; my head whirls. I try to reflect, but can only repeat: "Prisoner. I'm going to be taken prisoner." My one dread and horror!

Once more I thrust my head outside. There is nothing to be done; no means of passing. The road is ploughed up with projectiles. Returning, I tear up a few letters. All around me are none but Moroccans. The first shock passed, my presence of mind returns, and I clearly see what is going to take place: a rush of Germans into the grotto, the massacre of the wounded Moroccans, and of myself along with the rest. No, I prefer to die outside rather than in this hole. It can't be helped; I must try to reach the hospital.

Again I find myself at the entrance of the grotto. I measure the distance to be traversed: the most dangerous part is the crossing of the road. Afterwards, the tree-covered slope descends abruptly to Bucy; the balls will pass over my head.

There will also be shells coming crashing down, but I have no choice; if I stay here, I am done for.

Gathering up my remaining strength, I rush out. The road is crossed. I fling myself flat on to the ground, to recover my breath. Now I see Bucy and a part of the ravine. Shrapnel and projectiles are bursting on every side. I am perfectly calm; I do not miss an atom of the charm of the situation. But my chances are poor. Forward! I descend gently, holding on to the trees. My *musettes* are choking me. With my knife I cut the two straps. Ah! now I breathe better. Another effort; the first houses are in sight.

"You cannot pass here! Where are you going?"

"The lieutenant has authorized me to go down to Bucy."

"You're not wounded?"

"No."

"Then you cannot pass. Those are my orders."

He is a light infantry corporal, a finely built soldier, with a strong, obstinate expression on his face. He continues—

"I see you are in a sorry plight, but it was the commander himself who gave me my orders: 'Only the wounded are to pass.'"

"Very good. You are right. It's wrong of me to be ill."

I sit down by the corporal's side, partially protected by a bit of crumbling wall. He informs me that a terrible battle has been raging ever since the morning, that after an awful bombardment our first lines have been overthrown, and that we hold only the road which is on a level with the grottos. At any moment this last line may be broken through, and the Germans will then pour down on Bucy.

A perpetual stream of wounded. After a rapid inspection the corporal allows them to pass. The roar of cannon is deafening; it shows no signs of stopping. The balls sing above us, some crash into the ground: *ffuutt*....

"The thing that worries me most," remarks the corporal in confidential accents, "is that I have left my haversack up there with my watch in it. A silver watch! I'm dreadfully afraid I shall never see it again!"

I do not dare to confirm his fears.

I look anxiously in the direction of the ridge on which fighting is going on. My fatigue and weakness are such that I am almost indifferent to everything; there is but one settled determination in my mind: not to be taken prisoner.

An hour passes. The firing seems to be dying away. The wounded continue to stagger along to the hospital; they give us bad news.

"Ah! the deuce!" suddenly exclaims the corporal. "We are giving way!"

Actually we see small silhouettes come tumbling down the slope. This is the end; the line must have been broken.

"Off you go, if you are able to walk. There is no reason why you should stay here any longer. *Nom d'un chien*, if only I can get back my haversack!" he continues.

A rapid handshake and I move away. I proceed along one of the streets of Bucy, keeping close to the walls. Shells batter down on to the houses around. Another couple of hundred yards and I reach the hospital. Look out! A dangerous crossing, and a raking fire along this road. A company of Moroccans is in reserve: all the men side by side, leaning against the walls. They await the order to attack. With eyes fixed on me, they laugh and seem to be watching for the moment when I shall be bowled over like a rabbit.

No loitering here: either I shall get across or I shall not. Well, here goes! I dash forward and find myself in the hospital yard. Two shells explode on the stable. The major recognizes me.

"Ah! It's you, is it? Well, you're a lucky fellow! Come in, quick."

I lie down at the foot of the stairs, exhausted by my latest effort. I am so sleepy I can scarcely keep my eyes open.

Without a pause the major is signing evacuation orders.

"Clear out, fast, those who are able to walk. Bucy may be taken any moment."

The wounded go hobbling away along the grapeshot-riddled road, the balls giving forth their odious buzzing sound all the time. Two carts are harnessed, and in them a score of badly wounded men are heaped together.

As in a dream, I recognize comrades of the 352nd. They tell me that the 21st has been exterminated. Ah! And Belin? No one can give me any information.

"What of the 24th?"

"It was in reserve still a short time ago."

Where are my comrades? Poor fellows. Here comes Lieutenant R——, the lieutenant of my section. He is hopping on one leg, with a bullet in his thigh. No sooner do I see him than I ask—

"Where are my comrades?"

"Ah, yes, I know whom you mean. Well, all five were uninjured an hour ago. That's all I can tell you. Things are pretty hot!"

I help him to get into the cart.

"Are you not coming too?"

"No, *mon lieutenant*, I am not wounded."

"Good-night, then, and good luck."

I wait another hour. The ridge is still being held, otherwise the Germans would be here. I don't know where to put myself so as not to be in the way. I feel worse than I should with a bullet in my skin, but a sick man, surrounded by others suffering from bleeding wounds, must be aware that he is a bore and a nuisance.

An infantry sergeant, who has just been brought down on a stretcher, has a gaping wound in the abdomen, caused by a shell explosion. He wears a calm though sad expression, and scarcely seems to suffer at all; he simply turns his eyes to right and left, watching the movements of the attendant who is dressing the wound.

All the time cries and calls are heard alternating with the crash of explosions.

"You stretcher-bearers, go and fetch a cook who has just lost both his legs, close to the wash-house."

"And you others, don't stay in the yard; you'll get killed."

"The wounded, as they enter, must leave their rifles at the street-door."

The major perceives me, lying on the ground.

"See, here's an evacuation order. Off you go to Septmonts."

It is half-past four. As it is beginning to get dark the bombardment slackens. I grasp a few hands.

"*Au revoir*, old fellow. You'll get there all right."

I cross Bucy. Stupefied, the inhabitants stand at the doors. There are ruins everywhere. A few of the women are in tears. The road to Vénizel: four kilometres straight across the plain. My fevered excitement sustains me, along with the one obsessing idea: If only I can reach the bridge I shall not be caught.

The hours seem to drag along on leaden footsteps. In the distance I see a column on the march; they are reinforcements. At last! A battalion of Zouaves. Khaki-coloured *chechias*, infantry capotes and velvet trousers form their accoutrement; there is nothing about them of the classic Zouave. As I come up I salute the commander, and say to him—

"Make haste. They are still holding out up there."

"That's right; we'll soon be with them."

Boom! Four shrapnels right on the front section, on a level with which I find myself. No harm done, however.

It is getting dark. I continue to advance, somewhat shakily, but that matters little.

The bridge! I show my evacuation order to a captain. So gently does he say the words: "Pass, my dear fellow," that a scruple comes over me, and I say—

"I am not wounded, you know, I am only ill."

Vénizel. I meet Perron, the head stretcher-bearer of the 352nd. He is going to Billy, to bring away some wounded. He offers to accompany me, and takes my arm. Two more kilometres in the dark. Fortunately we know the country well. The cannon having stopped, the sudden silence is somewhat disconcerting. There is a buzzing sound in my ears.

Perron knows no one at Billy, so I take him to the people who found accommodation for us in October. They have not forgotten Lieutenant Roberty.

"He is surely not dead?" they ask.

"No, he has been evacuated."

"And your other friends?"

"Ah! yes, where are they? This morning they were still alive, but now——"

A man belonging to the 21st saw Belin about noon, engaged with his bayonet in the trenches. By questioning everybody, right and left, I learn that in all probability the 24th company has lost fewer men than any other of the regiment.

My hosts prepare a bed for Perron and one for myself. I can no longer see clearly, so I turn in and go to sleep.

Thursday, 14th January.

Twice in the night I awake with a start. Bare-footed and in my nightshirt, I run outside to listen. They are our own troops passing in the direction of Vénizel. The Germans will not cross the Aisne.

At eight in the morning I continue my way, with a wounded man belonging to the 21st. Billy is a very excited place.

I perceive Sergeant Chevalier of the 24th. At once he reassures me: Verrier, Reymond, Varlet, Maxence and Jacquard are safe and unhurt. The company has suffered but little: five or six killed, a score of wounded.

What a relief! I make my way towards Septmonts in almost a gay mood, half supporting the man of the 21st, who is wounded in the arm, and half supported by him. My companion tells me that he has been engaged in hand-to-hand fighting in the branches, and has fired point-blank on the Germans. The more they killed, however, the more there seemed to be left.

Unfortunately, no one can tell me anything of Belin!

At Septmonts an ambulance doctor examines me thoroughly.

"Good; I must pack you off to bed. Go and see Desprès."

Desprès has a small pavilion near the château, containing beds for about a score of sick and wounded. He is the hospital attendant. Busily engaged as he is, running from one bed to another, he gives me some food, and I speedily find myself tucked in between the white sheets. How calm and quiet it is here! I feel more tired and feeble than ever.

Sunday, 17th January.

For three days I have been resting here under the watchful care of Desprès, who bestows as much attention on his patients as would a mother. It puzzles me exceedingly how this excellent and kind-hearted fellow manages to get through his various duties. In the intervals of sweeping out the room, I learn that his wife lives in the neighbourhood of Montdidier, right in the heart of a bombarded district. The family is scattered; the home must be in ruins. He utters not a word of complaint, but devotes himself whole-heartedly to his task of soothing and consoling us.

Finally I receive news of my friends: a long letter from Reymond, brought by one of my wounded companions. He writes as follows—

"Well, you are an old humbug, giving us the slip in this fashion! Still, you're a lucky fellow, though now you must take good care of yourself. Perron informed us that you were at Septmonts. We have been ordered to take a rest, but our present surroundings are nothing to boast of. I myself am terribly lame, and my feet bleed a great deal. Verrier can scarcely breathe; his coughing is painful to listen to. Maxence, under an attack of acute dysentery, has that pretty green complexion you remember seeing when we were down at Fontenoy; Varlet's knee is as big as a child's head; Jacquard is laid up with bronchitis. We take up all the doctor's time, when he makes his rounds.

The regiment held its ground long enough to enable reinforcements to arrive. The whole of our squadron was there.

Belin is living. He came out without a scratch, though he fought like a madman. I'll see you again before long, old fellow...."

As I lie in my bed I read the letter again and again. This evening, I am able to get up and sit on the doorstep. The rain has stopped. How well I appreciate the peace and quiet of this place as I listen to the roar of the cannon and the crack of the rifles in the distance.

Lector House believes that a society develops through a two-fold approach of continuous learning and adaptation, which is derived from the study of classic literary works spread across the historic timeline of literature records. Therefore, we aim at reviving, repairing and redeveloping all those inaccessible or damaged but historically as well as culturally important literature across subjects so that the future generations may have an opportunity to study and learn from past works to embark upon a journey of creating a better future.

This book is a result of an effort made by Lector House towards making a contribution to the preservation and repair of original ancient works which might hold historical significance to the approach of continuous learning across subjects.

HAPPY READING & LEARNING!

LECTOR HOUSE LLP
E-MAIL: lectorpublishing@gmail.com